YOU MUST BE JOKING, LORD

YOU MUST BE JOKING, LORD

MICHAEL HOLLINGS
and
ETTA GULLICK

McCRIMMONS
Great Wakering Essex.

First published in Great Britain in 1975 by
Mayhew McCrimmon Ltd
Great Wakering Essex

This edition
© 1997 McCrimmon Publishing Company Ltd.

ISBN 0 85597 089 8

Printed in Hong Kong by
Permanent Typesetting & Printing Co. Ltd.

CONTENTS

Foreword	7
Introduction: You must be joking, Lord	9
You — You must be joking	12
Me	32
Him, Her, It	79
Us/We	101
Them	115
You — Knowing you in the heart	136
Index	155

FOREWORD

We can imagine some people saying: 'Another Hollings-Gullick book of prayers! You must be joking!'

Well, here it is!

For us it is not a joke. Rather it is real. It shows up the variety we find in our own lives and the lives of others, set as we all are in God's world, human beings touched by the divine.

We reach up and down. The sublime and the ridiculous are not poles apart. They are often the same person, the same happening, or the same event seen from different angles.

We can laugh at the clown; just as easily we can weep for and with the clown. We can see the crucifixion of Jesus Christ as ridiculous and grotesque – or as unutterable love challenging and elevating mankind.

If you read these pages, you may be caught up here, and offended there, made to cry with compassion, laugh in derision, or grin in sheer joy.

Many of the prayers are written with young people in mind, and often at their special and individual request. They have told us that using these prayers echoes their own doubts, fears, longing and love. We want to thank them because they have shared with us. We hope our sharing with them will help many other people of all ages..., because if mothers, fathers, teachers and elders do

7

not speak this language, they should at least try to understand it.

So we call upon the Spirit of the Lord to fill each and every person who reads this book. For he alone has the power to renew the face of the earth.

Feast of St. Richard   Michael Hollings
of Chichester   Etta Gullick
1975

This popular collection of Prayers has been reprinted at the request of so many people in memory of Michael Hollings and Etta Gullick.

YOU MUST BE JOKING, LORD

Why did you pick up this book and begin to look inside? Was it the attractive cover? The names of the authors? A sense of need for new prayers? An aimless browsing in a bookshop? Or was it the title of the book?

There are lots of other possibilities too, but we must fix upon the title.

Either you know the expression, and perhaps use it, or it may seem strange to you. In our experience, the phrase is used quite widely, but maybe only in a certain age range or in a particular social setting.

Anyhow, it is really an exclamation which sums up a mood of questioning, a sense of disbelief at a statement, a laughing brush-off to a suggestion made about one's opinion or ability to do something. And so on.

So we would want to think that this book is a book of *Faith*. Like us, like our faith, it is sometimes shallow, sometimes deep. Sometimes the spirit is acceptance, sometimes there is questioning and fighting against. We find ourselves following the swings and moods of the human being.

This we have learnt from the Psalmist — and from living. For the human being is fickle — as Jeremiah says:

'The heart is more devious than any other thing, perverse too; who can pierce its secrets?' (Jer. 17.9)

Fickle and faithful, because of the wonderful, fearful and beautiful make up of body, mind, heart and will. This God-created mixture can lie asleep, can explode in huge, destructive energy, or can be channelled to development of unbelievable goodness, power and love.

So we would think that this book is a book of *Love*.

Faith and love go very closely together. Unless we believe in God, we cannot really love him . . . we just mouth words. Unless we believe in people, we cannot really love them — him or her individually, them together.

But when we look at each other . . . think about believing and loving each other . . . we may well say: 'You must be joking, Lord!'

So, finally, we would think that this book is a book of *Hope*.

No matter how impossible,
> absurd,
> stupid,
> unbelievable — nothing is impossible with God.

So, in a sense, the life we have lived and live persuades us that the Lord God is not a terrible ogre, seated on a throne and casting thunderbolts about. Nor is he a distant computer adding up the pros and cons of all we do.

No, rather than these, he is Our Father . . .

	to be respected in
his power,	to be trusted in
his providence,	to be loved in
his love . . .	

and in all this both on earth and in heaven
there should be for each of us the
welling up of the Spirit in
the laughter of pure
love and joy . . .
and if this is not so, then the joke
is on us, Lord!

YOU — YOU MUST BE JOKING

Way back in history, so the researchers and scholars seem to tell us, our earlier ancestors were almost instinctively drawn to someone or something outside themselves. Over the centuries, at various times and in various places, this 'Other' has 'become known', 'been revealed', 'revealed himself', 'been spoken of by prophets' and so on.

His name is varied: God,
                                       Yahweh,
         The One, the Almighty.
         Creator.
         Holy.
         Thou.
         Father.
         Spirit.

And so today we are writing of him as

YOU.

Who is this You? What is he like? Is he, he? — or she? Is any language like that nonsense? Sometimes, what we hear or read or seem to understand is almost contradictory to what we read or hear or seem to understand at another time.

You — God — Lord — One — You seem to ask people impossible things. How can we understand you asking Abraham to kill his own son? Or saying we must hate mother and father and brother and sister? Where does it get us when you say we must die in order to live?

You see why we are tempted to say: 'You must be joking, Lord?'

But, somehow, we are to learn about you. We can listen, question you; try to understand the silence you speak; try to accept your touch of love, and how your love may seem like indifference, distance or even hatred.

As we live and move busily in this world, it is not easy to believe you first have been in communication — you opened the conversation — you loved us before we could even think.

You — God — have so often been hidden, and when you became visible in Jesus Christ, you were just as puzzling. You frightened your disciples when you were asleep in the boat and they thought you didn't care, and they were going to sink. You got them all mixed up over what you were trying to do, to the extent of Judas going off, fed up with you, to destroy what he could not possess.

Then you went away in death, and coming back, you went away again, saying this was the only way you could be with us till the end of time and through eternity.

So now —
You who know us first ... we must come to know you;
You who love us first ... we must come to love you;
You who serve us first ... we must serve you, at last.

The straight simple way is like a child's game of hide and seek, with the Lord leading the dance ... we might say 'leading us a pretty dance'! Is it, a man will ask now and again, just a stupid, senseless and cruel pastime for a spiteful spirit? In his bitter, lost and self-pitying moments, man may answer 'yes'.

But then, when anyone has the patience, the trust and the courage to love you, joy bubbles, thanks flows over and instead of feeling we are being laughed at, we begin to share your sense of humour. And then we know and love you well enough to say to you, as it were face to face, when you seem to ask some outrageous trust or obedience: You must be joking, Lord . . . and saying that, plod on with the prophets and the saints through the Divine madness which is You.

SHORT PRAYERS

Why . . . Why . . . Why, Lord . . . Why?

Love calls; only love can answer. How can I love you, Lord?

Be perfect as your Father is? You must be joking Lord!

I've known what it is to hate you Lord.
Teach me what it is to love you.

She said she loved me. You said you loved me, Lord.
Now she says she doesn't any more. Can I trust you to
go on loving, Lord?

Without you, I can do nothing.
But with you I don't seem to do much either!

I am miserable and hurt. Heal me, Lord!

Your ways are very strange, Lord.
I wish I understood what you are getting at !

Praise the Lord!
You pour out your Spirit abundantly.

Unfathomable,
impenetrable,
uncatchable you
– give yourself to me, Lord!

Thank you for being you!
Thank you for making me!

Good? You are great, Lord!

I woke up laughing, full of joy.
I know you were with me.
Thanks, Lord.

YOU MUST BE JOKING, LORD

I don't understand why you allowed pain, God-of-Love,
but I can't take much more. Help Lord . . . please.

The world is full of you, and I feel utterly empty and
alone.
Please, Lord, make a contact.

You must be joking, Lord

The news of Jesus Christ says: Peace on earth.
The news of the world says: War in the Middle East.
The news of Jesus Christ says: Peace to men of goodwill.
The B.B.C. says: Fifty Buddhist monks have been
    slaughtered.
The news of Jesus Christ says: The meek shall inherit
                the earth.
The Telstar programme is highlighting exploitation of
                the poor in Latin America.
The news of Jesus Christ says the meek shall inherit
                the earth.
The papers say a character called Rockefeller has three
                hundred and sixty-five million.
The news of Jesus Christ says happy are the poor in
                spirit for the kingdom of heaven is
                theirs
It's just as well, because some of the poor in spirit I
                know are being evicted tonight and others
                are dead scared of thugs on the underground.
The news of Jesus Christ says happy those who mourn
    because
                comfort will be theirs.

The pictures on TV show refugees weeping, flood victims
       weeping, bomb-blasted people weeping,
       starving people weeping, weeping, weeping . . .
And I could go on, couldn't I, Lord?
And that is why I sometimes say to myself (I'm rather
       afraid to say it out to you)
He must be joking!
But now I've plucked up courage, I'm facing you Lord,
I'm putting all this before you, I'm asking you what is
       going on?
Looking at the contradiction of what I've just thought,
       I have to say: – this time to your face –
You must be joking, Lord.

Believing, unbelieving

    I don't suppose I shall ever understand, Lord, why
you made men and women so that so much could go
wrong with them, and they could deliberately or by
stupidity cause so much hurt, harm and upset. I don't
understand, but I still try to trust you. Is this what they
call faith? Because, if so, it's the hardest test of stupidity
over common sense I've ever met! Lord, I still try to
believe. Help that part of me that can't believe!

YOU MUST BE JOKING, LORD

Lord, why do you hang there?

Of all the horrid signs, I think the most horrid is you on the cross, Lord. It seems revolting; it makes me sick. And apparently some people will sit and look at you strung up there on the cross, and go deep into this prayer-thing. But I just find it turns me off, makes me sick inside. I can't see the point, or why it was necessary. Did it really help? And if so, how? It's all so back-to-front and cruel. Can good come out of evil like that, because it was evil, what they did to you? If I had been with you, I think I would have called out as the others did: 'Come down from the cross; save yourself'. But you didn't, so I suppose there's something to it all, only I still don't understand. Can you let me see?

God is my Father

If I read you right, Jesus,
you are saying God is my father, and I must
love him, honour and obey him.
But you must be joking, Lord!
Have you ever met my father . . . that old bastard
who beats hell out of Mum,
who's drunk every Saturday night, after losing his wages
    on the horses
who says you're a laugh and whose favourite expletive is
'Christ'?
You must be joking, Lord . . . that's what I have for

a father-figure, as they say – a drunken, smelly,
vicious, gambling no-good, who doesn't love me, doesn't
even bother to hate me . . . just pushes me out of the
    way.
Is God, our Father, like this? How can I have an idea,
a picture, of 'father', which isn't coloured by my Dad?
I expect Joseph was all right to you, Lord . . . I expect
he loved and cared for your mother, Mary.
Did you ever see him drunk, Lord? Did he ever hit Mary,
    and
tell you to get lost? Did he spend what he earned (I
    suppose
he bothered to work) on some gambling, telling your
mother to – bleeding-well-make do on . . . nothing?
So, you see, Lord, I think you must be joking,
because I'm stuck with Dad, and so is Mum, and we make
do with him, and in a way we love him, but he's hell to
live with, Lord . . . !
And so I could see God as my friend, God as my mate,
    God as my Mum, my girl,
but I just can't get God as my Father, Lord.
So do you mind if I do it my own way? And think of all
the love I know and all the kindness and all the
friends and everything nice and good – and say:
you must be like that God the Father? –
or else you must be joking, Lord!

How can I trust you?

The bomb took all the family but me. How could
they, Lord? How could you? I can't forget, I can't

19

forgive. I hate with a deep and burning hate. How can I trust? How can I love? Lord . . . I'm desperate. Wash away the hurt in your love, wash away the pain in your pain, wash away the bitterness in your forgiveness, Lord. Forgive me, so that I can somehow begin to forgive, and then begin to love again.

Finding a place to be alone with you

We live in a little house, Lord, and it is full of people. We fall over each other, and never have a chance to be quiet and alone. Someone told me if I wanted to know you better and love you more, I must be still and alone at least a little bit each day. But I didn't see how I could be alone, until I thought of something, Lord, and I hope you won't be offended. You see I've come into the toilet and locked the door, and I am just sitting here thinking of you and talking to you. I hope it's all right by you, Lord, because it really is the only place I won't be disturbed, and so I think I'll try to make a habit of this each day, and ask you to bless me as I try to be alone with you.

Do you really love me?

Do you really love me, Lord? It is so hard to believe you do when you let this pain eat through me, and no doctor can do anything but try a new drug, tell me how well I look and promise to call next week. Do you really love me, Lord, to let me suffer like this? Oh, I know you, Jesus Christ, suffered on the cross. But that was only three hours, and I've been at this more than three years. Do you really love me, Lord? I wish I really knew you did. Perhaps you could take away just a little of this pain, or raise a corner of this curtain-blackness of my prayer . . . just to show me you really love me, Lord.

Praying from where I am

Lord, I have to start praying from where I am now, and often my prayers are about things that may seem unimportant, but that's because they are the kind of things I am involved with. What I am asking is that you should help me to grow by working through and by overcoming the small problems of life so that I will, with your help, be able to wrestle with more difficult problems and situations. Perhaps if I do this I will come to know you and myself more deeply? So give me faith and the Holy Spirit to guide and teach me what to ask for.

Thank you

Thank you for sunshine on wet leaves, for yesterday's smile, for the person who said 'Good morning', for a rose in a florist shop which spoke of you.

Thank you

Someone told me to take a leaf, and to go away by myself for a quarter of an hour and look at it. Silly, it sounded, but I thought I'd try, so I did. Do you know, Lord, it was a whole new world. I don't even know the name of the tree it came from, but after a bit it seemed the most beautiful leaf in all the world. It came out from the stem, green and delicate. I thought it looked a little like a hand, with veins all through it. Then near the edge it was just going golden, coming back into the green so finely, I can't quite say where the green and the gold began. It's beautiful, Lord, and if it shows something of the beauty of your mind, you must be terrific. Thank you for nature, Lord, and thank you for the person who made me stop and look at it.

Only you help me

Lord, it's hard to see why you allow so much misery and tragedy to hit us! Yet I know it's when I'm unhappy and lonely that I turn to you in a way I don't when things go well. This is just how I am! It's when I'm broken and hurt that I know that only you love me the whole time and that you will always be with me. Friends quickly leave someone who is a failure or who rebels against society. Job was lucky to have friends who told him where he'd gone wrong! At least they cared in some way! Mine just drift away and don't want to know about my problems or listen to my complaints. Thank you for being patient with my grumbles and my miserableness. I'm grateful that you put up with me when I'm at my most unattractive. Take my brokeness and use it and mend it if you can. I seem so useless, but in my funny way I do love you!

Glory be to you

Glory be to you, Lord, for apples and eggs.
Glory be to you, Lord, for bicycles and babies.
Glory be to you, Lord, for mothers and houses.
Glory be to you, Lord, for sun and wet paving stones.
Glory be to you, Lord, for dogs and leaves on trees.
Glory be to you, Lord, for stars and puddles that reflect them.
Glory be to you, Lord, for bread which feeds and grapes for wine.
Glory be to you, Lord, for man and for woman, life and death.
Glory be to you, Lord, for sleep and rest, energy and joy.
Glory be to you, Lord, for Jesus Christ, God-man, beloved.
Glory, glory, glory, glory, glory be to you, Lord. Amen.

Science fiction

One of the things I like doing, Lord, is reading science fiction. Some people laugh at me and say how I waste my time. But you know, Lord, I find it mind stretching and wonderful. As the authors take me out into the galaxy, put unthought problems and possibilities before me, and somehow widen and deepen my sense of your vastness, complexity and simplicity . . . I just sit in open wonder at you. My mind boggles, my heart leaps, and I find myself saying Amen, alleluia. You are Alpha and Omega. I don't really know what I'm saying, but it all comes pouring out. I speak from the deep part of me, a part that wonders and praises and is full of awe and joy. Alleluia. Praise you, Lord.

Conflicting love

All day I have been torn in different directions by love of you, and love of my daughter. Oh, I know they should be the same, somehow, but the trouble is I cannot see how you can let her suffer the way she does. How can you allow the doctors to do these things to her, and still scratch their heads? How is it despite my prayers, you do not let them find out what is wrong? You said ask and you will receive. But I have asked not for myself but for my daughter. And what have I received? Anxiety, disappointment, doubt of the doctors, doubt about their truth or lies to me, and no answer for my daughter. Lord I am torn by love for you and love for my daughter. How can I go on loving and trusting you, when she is like this? Lord, have mercy on us both.

Where is your answer to my prayer?

I got up this morning, all set for holiday,
going away in mid-summer, set for camping,
my girl and I, searching for the sun and openness and
    freedom,
Lord.
Me away from my factory, and she from the office.
She said to me last night . . . 'Say a prayer, Sid.'
Well, I admit I said 'Why?'.
'For good weather of course,' she said, 'just pray.'
And I felt a fool, but for her I said it . . .
'Lord, Sally and I,' that's me, Sid, 'are going on the bike
tomorrow . . . and will you make the sun shine and the
breeze be nice and cool as we speed along?'
Well, Lord, talk about 'coming down in buckets'
I think it's more like barrels . . . Ugh! Sheets,
barrels, buckets . . . the lot. Fantastic! Until
I have to shrug my shoulders at you and say:
'You must be joking, Lord!'

Then we got where we were going and there was this
geezer, Lord! My! He let us have it . . .
'No good-for-nothing-druggy-hippies in my field,'
he said. 'I'm not having you mucking around –
we're decent people, the Mrs and me!'
And, you see Lord, we aren't these things really . . .
Well, we've had the odd smoke, and we dress casual,
we go about a lot together though we aren't married
. . . but there isn't anything wrong, Lord . . . not
Wrong-wrong.

YOU MUST BE JOKING, LORD

So, where is your answer to my prayer Lord?
It's not in the weather, it doesn't seem to be in
this character ... unless you're joking, Lord?

And now my bird is kicking up and saying it's
all my fault, and she wishes she hadn't come.
So, what do I do? I'm asking you now, because
she's gone to sleep, and I feel very alone.
I began the whole holiday by praying ... as she
wanted me to ... but is there any point in it, Lord?
If I saw something coming out of it,
If only I felt good and humble and generous.
If I knew she was all right?
But I don't and I don't and I don't ... So
though I believe in you and I try to pray
I do not understand and again and again
the cry comes, however I put it away ... a cry
of lostness, Lord ... I cannot understand you, I
don't get your sense of humour, or your justice,
or your love ... so, lost as I am, I just try to trust you
when I say: 'You must be joking, Lord.'

Sharing my problems with you.

Lord, I am always bringing my problems to you,
because I know you care, and you listen. It often isn't
easy to realise that you are hearing when I begin to talk
to you, but after a little, somehow, though the problem
is still there, I have a sense of sharing it and it doesn't
seem so hard to live through. Somehow I know that you
are with me in my situation and that all will be well even
if it is heavy going. I do thank you for this, Lord.

God and the policeman

You know, Lord God, that I am a policeman?
It gives me a lot of heart when I think you know,
because
   it seems to me that we human beings treat you like
a policeman –
so, if you will forgive me saying so,
I have a fellow feeling with you.
What I mean is this –
Any time anyone wants something, and generally
   something difficult –
they call on you, they pray, they ask.
Most other times 'they' don't remember you exist, or
   worse –
they say they don't really believe in you and all that,
they are free men and women, they don't need that sort
   of thing.
Well, you know that's the way they treat a policeman –
(or policewoman for that matter) –
They suddenly ring us up, say there is an accident, an
emergency, death, a child stuck in the toilet –
come quick . . . help! . . . Other times in the street,
on the beat . . .
we might not be there, they look the other way,
or laugh or sneer . . .
sometimes they spit in the gutter.
Then when we're in plain clothes we hear them talking,
despising us, calling us names . . . the rest.
It seems so like the way they treated you, Lord.
And then another funny thing . . .

As soon as anything goes wrong,
they blame, you and us . . . because someone has
broken in, because their car is stolen, because,
in your case, a child is sick, an earthquake happens,
a man dies suddenly.
Lord, you bear this, you are patient, you are kind . . .
you love . . .
Give me patience, give me kindness, give me love. Amen.

Jesus, are you God?

It's hard to believe in you just now, Lord! I think I
do. Then friends say; 'Surely you can't believe that load
of old rubbish?' Jesus, they say, you were a good man, a
revolutionary perhaps, a kind of hero, but no God. Then
I wonder did you believe that you were God? You said
that you were the Son of man, and God was your Father,
but did you say you were God? I get very muddled!
Yet I believe you died to help us, and that you rose
again. What ever they may say, your disciples believed in
your resurrection and this amazing belief changed them.
I want to love and follow you, and having to take up a
cross and follow you doesn't worry me too much, it's the
uncertainty, the thought of being taken in by a fairy
story, a vast hoax. I don't mind their mocking . . . much.
But Lord, help my unbelief.

You promised peace

There always seems to be a war going on somewhere in the world. But you, Jesus, promised that you had come to give peace. So what am I to think? Why doesn't your gift work? They say you are all powerful and all loving. Surely you would not promise something you couldn't give? It's the kind of time when I sit down and think, and look around, and see the chaos and fighting and hatred. Then I think – 'Jesus, you promised peace'! It goes round and round in my head and I find myself saying: 'You must be joking, Lord.' But then I think you said you would give peace; 'not as the world gives it'. So, I'm in a muddle really about what that means. Is it deep down inside me, not outside? Will you help me to be quiet and at peace, even though the world is at war? And will you help others to be like that too? I find it hard to believe and understand, so perhaps, Lord, you will make me see and hear, if I am still and listen. Anyhow, I'm going to try that now.

You are always with me

Lord, it is good to know that you are always about. I know you are because you said that you would be with us 'til the end of the world. But it isn't easy to know that you are there, and I often wonder if you are, when I call out to you when I'm afraid or in danger. You don't seem to answer or do anything. Then, thinking back I wonder if I'd been able to go on and keep going if you hadn't been with me, strengthening me. So then, Lord, I realise you are always about, and it is wonderful to have you to call on. Never leave me, Lord!

You ask too much!

Lord, I'm finding following you hard. I thought I'd only to say, 'Yes, Lord, I'm going along with you' and everything would be wonderful. It was for a little and I thought this is fine, it's like being high, I don't have to do anything! But you want me to change, to stop thinking of myself, and always be thinking of you and your demands for others. Well, it just isn't me, Lord! I don't want to follow you if it is like this — but then having begun to know you, everything without you seems a bit dreary. I suppose I'll have to keep on, so help me a bit because I'm not used to doing hard, difficult things and like to take the easy way out. Give me some joy and peace to keep me going!

Your will

All right, if that is the way you want, I'll accept, even though it is against what I want. Help me then, if this is what you want, that I may accept even without understanding.

Forget it Lord!

Forget it, Lord! I know I prayed for it, and really wanted you to answer my prayer. But it is stupid, senseless, Lord. I know that now, and I really pray that you will not answer the first prayer of mine. Rather let me have the patience and the grace from you to soldier on in this bleak, blank period. I know, deep down, you will set me free. Lord, I wait in hope.

ME

I am I

I am myself.

I am me.

The last is not very good grammatically, but it somehow sounds easier than the others.

I am *me* underlines the fact that each of us is an individual. You, reading this, are an individual. Or, if you should be reading as a group, the group is made up of individuals. You have only to stop a moment to discuss this point, and you will find different voices raised with different points of view.

Well, then, in life, though I ought not to isolate myself from other people or from nature, I am in a certain sense alone. I am constantly with this person, this *me*. It is this *me* I share with other people, or refuse to share.

Therefore, this *me* is of great concern to me! And if I have any thought for others, what this *me* is like to them should concern me quite a bit.

If this section seems inward looking, self-centred — fine, that is what it is meant to be! We neglect ourselves at our peril, and quite often to the cost of others.

'Know yourself' may be a trite phrase. Taken literally, pondered upon, allowed the swell of pride and the emptiness of self-despair, it can help us to grow in the Lord as the Lord grows in us, remembering always that 'He must grow greater, I must grow smaller'. (John 3.30)

SHORT PRAYERS

Why Me, Lord?

Sometimes it causes me to tremble when I think how they crucified my Lord.

I'm all caught up in myself. Let me out, Lord, or I'll go mad.

Lord, I just can't believe you're good and kind! Are you? I'm miserable and hurt; help me, Lord!

War beats on my mind! Hatred bruises me! Violence baffles me! Have you abandoned your world, Lord?

Lord, you have touched me. I can't speak for joy. Alleluia!

Lord, I am afraid, be with me.

All men my brothers? Then I don't know what brotherly love is, Lord. I've a long way to go. Lead me.

My heart is broken, Lord. Why did you make people so cruel? How can I ever forgive?

Stop me, Lord, from only being interested in me.

YOU MUST BE JOKING, LORD

No surrender! But, Lord, I think I could surrender to
    you!

My whole being cries 'Glory'; my mind explodes with
    'Glory'; my heart beats out 'Glory', Glory be to the
    Father and to the Son and to the Holy Spirit. Amen.

No one has ever been through my agony. And I can't go
    through it either. Give me strength.

Help me to know who I am, Lord!

I ache all over; I ache all through. Lord, have mercy.

Why did you make me?

I wonder why you made me, Lord?
Perhaps it is vanity or that I just think
of me.
But anyhow, why did you allow me to be me — and
so silly?
You see, I get upset when someone is rude to me,
or snubs,
says I'm a fool or laughs at me.
I get really angry when they say I'm stupid,
probably because I know I am, and
that makes me angry . . . but then I ask myself;
why did God make me this way, and I say to myself . . .
    and you . . .
You must be joking, Lord!

I see other people who are beautiful . . .
well, I'm not.
I see other people who win scholarships and are a
    success . . .
well, I'm not.
I see people who marry and make money, have a
    home . . .
well I'm single, I've no money, I live in a bed-sit.
So when I look at them and look at me, I get sad and say:
You must be joking Lord!
Perhaps you are, but then
perhaps the whole of life is a joke, and I am in on that?
Because, I think you must have a sense of humour, Lord,
and that's why I say:
You must be joking Lord!
But, like a clown, there's sadness in the clowning,
there's loneliness and suffering, there's
me . . . and you!
And you are God Almighty, King of the Universe,
and yet you're strung up on a tree to die . . .
You must be joking, Lord! And we would call that
a sick joke . . . I mean
it has no taste, no sense, no beauty . . .
O.K! I don't understand! To me it's sick! So will you
tell me what it means? . . . and then perhaps
I'll understand the joke that's me,
and learn to laugh until I see
that when I say: You must be joking Lord,
it's me that is the joke, —
and you joke kindly, wanting me to join —
for it is only when

YOU MUST BE JOKING, LORD

I learn to laugh at me – your joke, Lord . . . that
I really come alive and laugh
with you who are my Lord, my King, my Love.

Has life a purpose?

Lord, people appear to have no purpose in life. The
whole world seems aimless. Lord have you a plan for the
world? If you have could you give me some idea what it
is? Scripture suggests that we should love you with all our
hearts and that we were made to love you, but how do I
begin to do this? I want life to have an aim so show me
what you want me to do, and then I'll be able to get on
with it and perhaps help others to do this too.

I'm not O.K.

I'm not O.K., Lord . . .
or so they've always told me.
I wear my hair long, I look dirty
I'm not O.K., Lord.
When I make a friend, she's
not O.K., Lord.
But my big brother,
he's O.K., Lord.
And my little sister,
she's O.K., Lord.
And their friends are
O.K., Lord.

That's what Mum and Dad say.
They are clever at school, they
make nice friends, they like
making their beds, and going to church
and doing home-work – they even come in
at night on time – They're O.K., Lord.
But it's different NOT being O.K., Lord.
I want so much to love my mother, but
it always goes all wrong and ends in quarrelling.
I want to love my father,
but he just reads the paper, and has no time,
and only says I'm lazy.
Well, I am Lord, but can't you tell him that
is not the thing to say? Why can't he love me,
even if I am lazy? Tell him I'm just
a little bit O.K., Lord . . . please!
And then YOU, Lord. I want to
love you too. But I suppose I'm
not O.K. with you, Lord, because
I don't like going to church; it's boring and
it isn't me. I swear sometimes . . .
who doesn't. Lord? I've stolen, lied
cheated, slept with girls . . . I suppose on that
I'm just not O.K., Lord?
That is, O.K. by you Lord (because
I don't care about the others, if you
understand me, Lord.)
You see I want to do good things . . . I
dug an old lady's garden once. It was
great! And I walked for a charity thing.
My feet were sore and I ached all over,

but that was great too, Lord!
If that's O.K., why am I just not
O.K.? Can't I love you and people
by doing things and being me?
I don't think your Mother, Mary,
understood you, but you had to
go on being you. Then others
didn't understand, and even hated you.
They didn't think you were O.K., so
they sneered and spat and beat and killed you.

That helps me, Lord! So perhaps, if
I keep on trying, and accept them
thinking I'm not O.K., somehow
you'll lead me through,
because I feel you understand,
and you'll go on loving me, if I try,
even though I'm not O.K.

. . . .

God says: You are O.K. lad, by me, because I made you,
and I love you. I know your problems, I know where you
go wrong . . . and I know what's right with you too.
So — Go on trying, lad-whom-I-love . . . because I love
you,
You're O.K. and anyhow I'll go on loving you. What
about
you loving me and thinking I'm O.K?

Pulling myself together.

Lord, help me. My mind and my feelings are going in all directions and I don't seem to be in control any more. People keep telling me to 'pull myself together', but that's just the trouble I don't have any 'together'! I'm all in bits and pieces that won't go together but pull in different directions. Lord make me simply trust that you will take all the bits and gently bring them together if I keep asking for your help. So help, Lord, help!

Have I an identity?

Lord, I don't know what I am really like. I put on a different face and outlook with each person I am with. I am the good son, obedient and biddable when I am with my mother, agreeing with her opinions. I am bright and rebellious with my friends at work; boastful and showing off when I'm with girls. When I am alone with no one about I don't know which me is the real one and it is frightening, so I turn on the radio and identify with the mood of the singers. Is there a me or just a collection of disguises and masks with emptiness behind? Help, Lord! Give me a glimpse of what you would like me to be and strength to become it; if I put on the appearance other people expect of me, surely I can take on the reality you want me to have? Give me the courage to follow your Son and become like him, for I think this is the only way I will find myself.

YOU MUST BE JOKING, LORD

Who am I?

Lord, I find it hard to discover what I'm like and if I exist apart from other people. Mum says it's part of growing up, and even at her age she feels incomplete, not a whole person! It seems odd to me! Help me to find out what I'm like and what you want me to be, for I think only you can help me to grow into a real person. I look at you in the gospels and believe if I could only follow you, all would be well. Show me how to start, and how to come to that peace that never seemed to leave you even in the crises of your earthly life. So, help me now, Lord.

God's work of art.

Paul, writing to the people of Ephesus said: 'We are God's work of art'. I think that is a good thought, Lord. Not just that others are, but I am your work of art – with all my funny lines and angles and bulges – ME . . . a work of art. You see, Lord, it gives me a kind of confidence, because they say I'm ugly and stupid and slow – and Oh, all sorts of horrid things.

But if I'm really 'God's work of art', then I know people are not always right, and God sees beauty differently. So now, not only me, but my brother John who is a spastic, and my friend's sister who is mongoloid, and that poor old man who shuffles round and waves his stick at kids on the pedestrian crossing . . . and so many others . . . they are 'God's work of art' too.

Because of this thought, how much joy and hope there is for anyone and everyone . . . and not just bye and bye, pie in the sky, but now, because your art is a living, growing wonder. Yet I know it can be spoiled by hatred and greed, and anger, and selfish me.

So help me, Lord, to see beauty as you see it in things and people, even when I think they're ugly. Help me to preserve and develop beauty in things, in people and in myself. Amen.

Adopted

I always thought they were my Mum and Dad, until someone let it out . . . I'm adopted, Lord! I don't know my mother or my father. 'They' say they don't know either. So what do I do? I hate 'them' for hiding it from me, and stealing my love. And then I love them because they *have* loved me, and they *have* looked after me. But why couldn't they tell me? And who were my *own* father and mother? What happened? Why was I left? Where are they now? Shall I ever know? O Lord, it's hard, and I can say 'You don't know what it's like, not even to have your own name, not to have anyone who is 'mine'! Since I heard, I've cried myself to sleep each night, and in the day, it's a sort of cloud over all I do. I know I'm being silly, I know I must face up to what is the fact of my life. But I don't see how I can do it. What's the answer, Lord?

YOU MUST BE JOKING, LORD

I'm nobbly, Lord

Why is it that you have made me nobbly, Lord?
Others seem so smooth and round and well finished.
When I say I'm nobbly I mean that in several ways.
My knees and elbows, but in a way
my face is too . . . very odd!
Then my voice is funny . . . nobbly,
I'd call it, Lord. You see
it doesn't come out evenly,
but it seems to have bumps in it,
and goes squeaky when I'm excited.
Perhaps the worst thing is that
the way I behave is nobbly –
I get up against people – somehow
rub them up the wrong way.
If I look at another person, I see
all kinds of failings and things to criticise.
And then I don't stay silent –
I criticise, though I know I shouldn't.
Why can I not control my tongue and
my mind?
In school, the teachers said I was
awkward – I'd call it nobbly, Lord.
At work, now, they say I'm a difficult
character,
or can't work with others, am a loner –
I just think I'm nobbly, Lord.
And so I want to ask you for help,
because I think I'm nobbly with you too, Lord.
I don't really see eye to eye with you about

the way you run this world. I think you
treat some people pretty rottenly. I don't
like priests and ministers and bishops and
I don't like pi-osity – ugh! But I'm not sure
you like it either, Lord – at least I hope
you've got more sense! So I want
to ask your help, Lord. If I am right
at all on anything, then help me not to be so
nobbly. I don't expect you to change
my face. I'll get on with that, and my body.
But really it's my mind and heart – the inner
me. I feel, Lord, you could soften me with your
Spirit; I believe (though I don't know if I
can trust you)
that you could help me to be understanding,
and less critical. I think you care enough
for me, in spite of all my nobbly-ness,
to smooth me out a bit.
Yet, Lord, if you do, and if it's good –
just leave me a nobble or two –
or somehow I feel,
it just won't be me any more, and I must
be me, nobbles and all, if necessary.
So, perhaps what I am saying is;
Lord help me to be me . . . and if 'me'
is nobbly, then, Lord, still help me to be just nobbly me!

YOU MUST BE JOKING, LORD

What shall I do?

It is the last term at school, Lord, and in a few weeks time I will be free. I've been longing for that day, Lord. Most of all I want to get away from books and classes and homework and all the petty rules. But, now, Lord, what shall I do? Whichever way I look, I don't really want to do what I see. I don't think I have much interest, Lord. I'd like to marry, but that isn't exactly work. I think I'd like to work with people, but that seems to mean more classes and exams and qualifications. Of course sometimes I would like to be a pop star or on the films. But what do I *really* want to do? I suppose deep down it's really marriage I want, and a home and children . . . a little group of people very close whom I can love and look after. Well, you see the muddle I'm in, Lord, so if I try to think it out and also to pray, will you send your Spirit of wisdom and counsel to help me to see the way ahead. Amen.

School nightmare

Lord, I'm scared, I
get lost, far more than once,
everyday!
The passages are all
like each other,
faceless, unfriendly.
They bewilder me,
terrify me.

I panic.
The doors in the passages
look the same.
They have no identity either.
Somewhere in this jungle
is the room where I should be.
I ask a boy, where?
But he jeers 'fool
find your own way,
find your own classroom.'
Where is it?
Where, Lord, where?
Unending passages
rooms that seem the same,
full of noisy creatures,
only interested in themselves;
No one cares about me,
not even the teachers.
Lord, I'm scared, and
I stay scared; even in the night
I wake up screaming, 'where?'
'Where?' I'm lost.
Help, Lord, help!
Stop me panicking
Show me the way. It's
the fear of being lost
that gets me.
Help, help, save me
from this hell of endless corridors,
of faceless rooms and of people who
just don't want to
know, me!

YOU MUST BE JOKING, LORD

I'm scared going to school

On the bus coming back from school, boys sometimes get beaten-up, Lord. It's happened twice to me. The boys from another school come up in a gang, and if I and another boy are almost alone, they just corner us and hit and kick us. So I'm dead scared, and often walk or even run most of the way home instead of catching the bus. I want you to protect me, Lord, and them that seems chicken. Perhaps you could just help me not to be scared, Lord? Or make the other boys stop. I don't know what, but do something, Lord, because I'm getting to hate going to school, and the bus-ride back hangs over me all day. Do something, Lord.

Why must I stay at school?

Jesus, I'm feeling really rebellious. They want me to stay on at school and do 'A' levels, but my friends are leaving to get jobs. They'll have a life of their own and money to spend. It just isn't fair that they can make me stay on at school, wearing this grotty uniform and doing dull work. They say I'll get a better job with 'A' levels. But it's now I'm thinking of, Lord. Anything can happen in the next two years! I could be really living and enjoying myself. I suppose you were obedient to your parents for longer than sixteen years; didn't you mind staying at home when you knew you'd other things to do? Help me to understand their point of view, and if I am to stay at school give me patience, and make the work a bit more interesting!

Growing up

Lord, I'm six feet tall, I'm a young man, and
I'm fifteen.
The other day, at a disco,
a girl asked me if I was married yet!
It made me feel terrific, Lord. She
thought I might be married! It's a
laugh really — at fifteen. But then she
didn't know how old I am, and it makes me
feel terrific that she thought I might be married!
I spent the rest of the evening, Lord,
sort of wandering about and dancing as a man,
thinking the others were only kids, but I
might be married.
And then I went home . . . and Oh dear Lord!
Mum said a child of my age should be in by nine o'clock;
Dad said he'd give me a good hiding if I went
to another disco . . . and I was too young for girls
    anyhow.
He said I should be interested in my lessons and football
and leave girls for men.
Football! Well, yes, it's all right . . . it's brilliant . . . but
girls are girls, Lord . . .
You made them that way. You know!
And she thought I was old enough to be married . . .
So it hurts to come home and be a child, be treated like
a ten year old. When can I grow up, Lord?
It's all right for them. They have forgotten what it was
like, but I am in it, Lord, right in it: and
the way Dad's going on I'll never be allowed a disco

or a girl . . . even if I'm eighteen.
So I just don't know . . . Make me patient. Make me
calm like some old people are. Stop me flying off
at Dad or Mum . . . But Lord, can you tell them I'm a
    man?

Help me to be myself

I was sitting on the sand this afternoon, Lord, and the
sea was coming in. A small boy was making a castle in
sand, building it against the sea. When the little waves
began to swirl round his castle battlements, I wanted to
go and help; I wanted to beat the tide, Lord . . . in a way
I wanted to beat you. I suppose it is because you are so
strong, and I am so weak; because you seem to mock
me sometimes. But then I was afraid to go and help him,
in case he thought I was mad, or laughed at me. I thought
too of the grown-ups watching. When you are a teenager,
Lord, it is so hard to be yourself (whoever that is . . . I
don't know) and yet keep up a front for others to see.
I wish I could be me without fear. Lord, take away my
fear . . . let me do 'mad' things like helping that small
boy, or helping a beggar or even being nice at home,
where they'd think I'd gone crackers if I did the washing
up . . . Lord help me to be myself!

Uncontrollable anger

I have a great angry feeling and a great hate, but I don't know why! All I know is that I want to go out and hurt somebody or something. This feeling seems to possess me, and I am terrified by it. How do I use this great force without damaging others? I'm not sure how! By kicking a football, chopping wood for the old . . . don't make me laugh, Lord. Show me what to do . . . something constructively destructive! Help me to use my passion and drive, and don't let *it* control me, Lord.

Bad thoughts

It's strange this mind you gave me, Lord! I set it to think of you, and it is restive until all of a sudden, it gets caught up in girls, or sex . . . and it's away . . . you're out of it, Lord. That's prayer . . . but then there's other times . . . into the light of joy, beauty, love, care — and into the darkness of despair, dirt, hatred, ugliness. So . . . is this a big joke, Lord . . . or just me?

Does everyone have the same trouble, or am I worst of all the world?

How is it, some can be calm, recollected, at peace — when I am at war in myself?

Well . . . here I am Lord! I'm trying now to be with you, and already I'm full of odd thoughts . . . so what, Lord — so what?

YOU MUST BE JOKING, LORD

Exams

I've got this exam Lord, and I know I haven't worked hard enough. But I'm trying now, a bit late, I admit, but I'm trying. I suppose it's unfair to ask ... but help me, Lord, because I've been a fool, and so much depends on this exam.

Exams

Lord, help me with my exams. My tummy is all churned up and my mind is in a tizzy. Help me to calm down. Give me your peace, and make me look at the questions without panicking — and so be able to work out calmly which I know most about. Panic and my tummy are the worst problems, so please soothe me and help me to use the knowledge I have in the best way possible.

Must I?

But, I don't want to, Lord! Why should I? Am I not free to do what I want. Must I always give in? Must I always say 'yes' when I mean 'no'? I thought we were free, Lord? Didn't you make us free? So why all this 'You must' business all the time? Why must I, if I don't want to, don't feel like it, think it is wrong? Why, why, why? Oh, all right, I know I get up-tight and irritable ... but at least I'm still talking to you, Lord, and most of my friends have given up long ago . . . so what about it, Lord? I really don't want to. Must I? Tell me somehow, I beg you Lord.

Work

Lord, my mother is always telling me to work hard, but I'm not sure why. Not many of the others do. The people in the Bible seemed to think you wanted them to work hard, and they seemed to find work satisfying. I don't think it's any fun keeping on doing something you don't like, but if you really want me to, I'll try! Perhaps you'll show me why it's a good thing, because I don't just get it, Lord!

I've passed!

Lord, I don't know how to say it. I'm over the top. I did try, I did work, but somehow I never thought I'd make it. Now I've passed my exams, I can go on, I'm on my way. It's great, Lord, it's really great. Thanks a lot Lord. I mean it.

I hate waiting

I've spent all day waiting, Lord. When I went to work the bus was late, then the train was late. I waited in the rain at the bus stop, and in a draught at the station. In the office it was one of those days, Lord, when nothing happens, and I really waited all day long, until I could shout for boredom and frustration. If I looked at my watch once, I looked at it a hundred times! It stood still. I hate waiting, Lord, and so much of life is waiting . . . and it was the same coming home. And now I'm waiting for you, and you don't seem to be about; and I hate waiting, Lord. Can't you make things happen more, or teach me how to wait . . . to wait in a way that is useful, prayerful . . . that would be it. But, I can't learn by myself, so I'm going on waiting for you to teach me, Lord!

I'm afraid of people

Lord I'm so afraid of people that I can't think of anything to say to them, but go all shut up inside myself. Help me to relax. Make me realise that they may be as unsure of themselves as I am and need encouraging to talk like me. Give me the right words to say. Put love in my heart instead of fear so that I will have the courage to speak!

I am alone

Lord, I am alone, I have no one who cares and I feel afraid and lost. You had a family and friends like Martha and Lazarus, so you knew the warmth of human companionship and the joy of people accepting you as you were. Did you ever know the loneliness of no one caring or wanting you? Perhaps you did when they all forsook you and fled? But you knew you were to die, so it wouldn't last long, yet you must have known something of the feeling of not belonging. Anyway, I know you understand my unhappiness, and I know you do care about me. This is the only thing that keeps me going on. It gives me hope and something of the warmth and sense of security that loving friends must give. Never leave me, Lord, and always keep me hopeful!

Mixed up love and hate

Lord, I can't understand how I love someone, yet sometimes hate them too. Hating and loving mix together in me. It's no help saying that it's because I love so deeply that the very depth of feeling enables me to hate as well. Perhaps it's because it is not a superficial love that hate comes in — but that's no comfort, no excuse, Lord. Perhaps Judas loved you so much that when he felt you were letting him, and God down, he betrayed you. I want to love and don't want to hate, but you've made hate and love so close together that sometimes I can't separate them. Then Lord, I look at you and wonder if you are having a joke at my expense? Surely, Lord, you must be joking!

I've got a spot coming!

Lord, I'm in a tizzy! I've got a spot coming on my face and I've got this date with my boy-friend tonight. Lord, please make it go away, or at least don't let it get any bigger! I want to look my very best and be my best self but I'll be worrying about it if it stays. It's very important so do do something, Lord, to help!

Untidy

Lord, why did you make me so untidy? Mum goes on at me for leaving things all over the place, just dropping my clothes on the floor when I undress, taking things out of cupboards and not putting them back. I get fed up with hearing this! It's hard for me to remember to put things away — I'm always in a rush or else I forget! Mum often puts them away in the end, so perhaps I don't really try.

Could you perhaps help me to make a start at being tidy, and make me see that it's important and that I do cause trouble to others by being untidy. I've heard this so often that it doesn't get through to me — make it somehow, Lord.

The pill

Lord, my friends who are engaged or have a regular boy-friend take the pill. My mother keeps on and on telling me it's wrong but I don't see why. Everyone else does! We really mean to marry when we can afford a house, but it may be years before we can, so why not? My mother says too, that the pill may be dangerous, may have an effect on the children we have, but we may never be able to afford to have any children! Life is so uncertain, why should we not enjoy loving each other now? The Church does not allow 'pre-marital intercourse' I know, but you, Jesus, said we were to love each other — show me what to do now, Lord, for I love him and I truly love you too!

I've done wrong

Lord, I have done wrong and I knew I was doing wrong when I had sex with my boy-friend. I never really wanted to and I didn't like it at all, but the other girls laugh at me if I don't. I'm going to stop now however much they jeer, so give me courage. I think I hate it because I don't love or respect the boys and it's just a kind of mechanical act. I am worried that sex in marriage might be like this — please, Lord, don't let it be. Help me to discover someone to love with my whole being, and give me strength not to do everything the gang does, specially when I know I am doing wrong. Amen.

I'm in love

All the world is bursting! O God I love you. I've never been like this before ! I see beauty in faces, I love people, I am in love. That's it Lord . . . I'm in love. Oh thank you, Lord, because I never knew what it was to be in love. I talked about it, I pretended to know. I didn't . . . not really. And now I do know, and it's wonderful, Lord, and the world is bursting. Alleluia. Amen.

I don't want to marry

Lord, I don't want to marry. Marriage seems to make chains that bind people together so that they can't be themselves. They get twisted, and hurt each other, and change from being loving people into frustrated men and women. I don't want to get like this, so I'd rather live with my boy-friend in freedom, but the church says this is wrong. Lord, what do you want of me? If you really want us to marry show us how we can stay loving and yet free within the bonds of marriage?

Loving in the right way

I went out tonight, Lord, with a wonderful girl. I can't put it into words. I can only say she was 'IT'. You know, Lord, all of me went out to her. If she had not been so good, I don't know where it would all have ended . . . except I think I know, because I know what I wanted. But, thank you, Lord. I was praying today, and I knew you would be about, and somehow, I don't know how, I had the strength to love her and stay right with her; to kiss her and go no further; to caress her, and not to seduce her. And now, I just want to thank you.

Are sex and love the same?

Lord, they seem to talk about sex the whole time! They read books, look at pictures in glossy mags, and then go to the cinema to see more! Are sex and love the same? The boys say try it and see; Mum says wait till you're really in love because it's something special; the telly sometimes makes it seem ordinary and dull; Church makes it something to feel guilty about; teachers make it just another part of science and rather clinical.

Lord, I'm in a muddle. What's love about, is it just something to do with the body? Is it like being hungry, thirsty, sleepy? There must be more to it than this! Surely loving is caring too, friendship, companionship, enjoying things together, sharing beauty, and sex is not just the satisfying of an appetite, but is mysterious and important? Help me see how love and sex go together and to discover how you want me to love, and whether Mum is right about it being something special!

Getting married in church

Lord, I want to get married in a fabulous white dress in church and have bridesmaids, organ music and singing, and photos of him and me taken in the porch. Church is much more glamorous than the register office.

But my Mum says this isn't honest as she doesn't think I'll go to church again after I'm married. Well Lord, I just don't know! I can't commit myself yet; I don't know what he'll want. We may be busy at other things on Sunday. It could be that getting married in church could change us and add something to our loving. Isn't it a bit up to you as well as to me? Any way help me to know what to do that will be fair to you!

Pregnant Father

Liz, my wife, is expecting Lord, . . . and very soon now. They say I've got to be there with her when it happens, and this is what's so odd, Lord. You see, as Liz began to swell, I felt her and loved her. First I thought how awful . . . she was getting all out of shape. Then, it was somehow lovely, and I was happy, and I thought she was lovely . . . I've never seen her so lovely, though my Liz cried a little and said she was ashamed to come out with me, looking like that. And I persuaded her, Lord. I said it was great, and she was great, and I was proud to be with her and say 'It' was mine and we were together.

But now it's all different somehow. She might die, or the child might die. Suppose something awful happened and the child was mongoloid? Would we live through this together, Lord, or would I disown her and 'it'? I've tried to work it out. I thought I couldn't bear it . . . perhaps I still do . . . I've just got to wait and hope . . . and if 'it' is mongoloid, Lord, give me strength. But then, suppose Liz dies? It could happen, couldn't it? What would I do? Go berserk? Run away? I just don't know and that is why I'm chewing my nails and talking to you. It could be . . . but then surely she will be all right?

I'm praying now, Lord . . . I want you to make it all right . . . I don't want a mongoloid, I don't want a spastic, I don't want Liz to die. So, Lord . . . that is me asking. God knows (I'm sorry I mean that) God knows I want it to live and Liz to live and all to be well . . . But, if it isn't and if Liz isn't and all the awful possibilities . . . O stop the worrying Lord and I will try to say and go on saying . . . though I don't understand and I don't know how . . . 'Not my will but yours be done'. AMEN.

I'm a teenager no longer!

It's just hit me, I don't understand what they are jabbering about! Talk about a generation gap — they are only two or three years younger than me! A year ago I was a teenager, but now I've steady work I'm part of the establishment. I don't seem to be able to communicate with them now. It's daft! They think I've sold out to the system. It's really shattering, Lord.

I can't get my discoveries about life over to them; can't show them that you can reform the system from inside and that somehow you've got to join them to beat them; that you have to be strongly rooted in you to do

59

this, and to be strongly rooted needs discipline. It's hard to preach self-discipline to would-be rebels; it's hard to put over that you have to die yourself so as to live more fully. Yet they would go all out training for a game of football, or would practise if they played in a 'group'. Help me, Lord, to put my discoveries about life to them and show them that they will have to make the break sometime, else they will be like children that never grow up. It's really hard changing, so please give them ears to hear and me a tongue to speak in a way they will understand.

I'm a soldier

There was a time, Lord, when I was just a nobody.
My pals knew me as Joe Soap, I worked for Woolworths.
Then I got fed up. I wanted adventure, excitement, to be
Somebody.
So I did what my pals said was suicide . . . I joined the
Army.
And was I somebody, Lord? Yes, right away I was
'You there, wake up!' 'You there, get a move on'; 'You
there, get your hair cut'.
So I became 'You', Lord . . . a person, real, but a
THING,
to push and shove and shout at and curse.
And then the time came. I was sent to be a real
soldier in the front line.
Only, the front line was disciplining ordinary people,
the front line was defusing bombs,

the front line was searching houses, where men and
women
were in bed together, and had never done anyone any
    harm.
But then downstairs in another flat
we found explosives and guns and
— so what do we do? The innocent
and guilty all mixed up —
And me in the middle, shot at,
sneered at, stoned, derided — a
bit like you, Lord, only I'm not all that innocent.

I'm somebody now — I'm
Tommy-go-home.
I'm Fascist Tommy.
I'm Tommy-the-thug.
Sometimes I'm nice Tommy.
Sometimes I'm Tommy-the-saviour.
Oh dear Lord, you said he who
took to the sword would die by the sword.
And I've taken it and it gets
me all mixed up. I'm not
making war, I'm trying to
make peace. But whose
side I'm on and who is
right, and where is the end?
I want to be kind, I want to
help Lord, but it is getting me
down. I hate being hated — I can't take much more —
so please, Lord, give me strength and
patience and love in the middle of hate.
Give us all your peace. Amen.

YOU MUST BE JOKING, LORD

Did I kill my friend?

Lord, help me in this great loneliness. I am shut in with the thought that my careless driving killed him. I keep thinking what I could have done to stop it happening, and keep wishing that I had died instead. His mother blames me. These thoughts go round and round in my head and no one can comfort me, or reach me in my misery. Let me know that you are with me and that you understand my unhappiness and sense of guilt. Lord, help me to learn to live with it; share with me the bearing of the burden so that it does not break me completely. Show me how to be sympathetic with those who are also isolated from others by their own particular kind of misery. Do not leave us on our own but be with us and support us, Lord.

I'd like to be attractive

Lord how do I become attractive like the girls in the glossy mags who have so many dates. I've tried eye-shadow, conditioning cream, mascara, new lipsticks but I stay just plain and rather messy! I've tried slimming and remain plump which is polite for fat! Lord, help me to be attractive. It comes to me that nowadays the fancy packaging has become more important than what's in it, and I wonder if this doesn't happen with girls. Is it silly to ask you to help me become attractive deep down and not just cosmetic deep?

Why am I bitchy?

Lord, you know I'm a mother with a family I love. And I think we really love each other in a tremendous way. But I want to moan at you, Lord, because every morning . . . or almost every morning . . . I'm so bitchy, I just let fly at all of them. If something is wrong I point it out, but what is worse, if nothing is really wrong I seem almost to make up a grievance . . . empty beer cans left by the boys, games not put away by the little ones, cigarette ash and butt ends all over the place (even if there is just one!). So what have you made me like this for, Lord? Why can't I relax, accept the mess, smile, laugh, tell-off gently . . . why must I be so bitchy, Lord?

I live in the City, Lord

I live in the City, Lord, and I want to say thank you.

You see, someone took me into the country. It was a great big place, full of silence, terrifying. The first night, I woke up in bed. The moon came through the window, it was all white, and something made a fearful hooting sound . . . I was all shivery and hid under the blanket and I prayed that night, Lord, against ghosts and animals and burglars and just being so quiet and alone.

But now I thank you Lord, because, I've looked at the moon in the middle of the night, and its white light is beautiful. I've heard that hooting again and it is no longer fearful . . .

It's an owl, Lord, and I've seen it, and I never thought I'd see an owl . . . gosh, an owl's great, Lord! It looks so wise and sleepy and old and like the judge in the court when my brother Sid was put down for drugs . . . only I'm not sure the owl isn't kinder than the judge, Lord. And now I've seen piglets; and wheat . . . you know, we make bread from that, Lord. I'd only seen Mother's Pride and Hovis! I thought the wheat was awfully dirty, but it looked good in the field, and the home-made bread . . . Gosh!

Then there was everything else, but I expect you know about it Lord, because you made it, didn't you? But, I thought you'd like to know I loved it, because sometimes I think, Lord in the middle of the city, perhaps no one really cares, and perhaps no one says thank you for the things out of tins, because, I think, they don't understand that you made everything Lord . . . the wheat and the piglets, and all that's in the tins — the moon and the owl, and you made me and them, Lord . . . the people who do not care and do not see . . . Oh, yes!

I must say thank you, Lord.

On the beat

When I was a kid at school, Lord, my Mum got
knocked down by a bus. I was with her.
It was awful, Lord, I'll never forget . . . blood . . .
Mum, my mum, on the ground . . . not talking . . . dead!

I didn't know she was alive, Lord, I thought she was dead!
I fell on her, cried on her, screamed!
They couldn't get me off . . . It was all horrible, a
    nightmare.
But then, Lord, there was this policeman, a bobby,
I don't know how he did it, but
he comforted me, got me straight.
He made a big impression on me, Lord, so I said:
'When I'm big, I'm going to be a policeman.'
I meant it, Lord, and . . . now I'm a policeman, a bobby.
But Lord, I never knew . . .
My Dad cursed me . . . said I was a sucker, accused me
of things I did not understand.
My girl said that was it . . . curtains . . . ugh!
But, I went on, Lord, and I'm still at it, only I don't
    understand.
People who ask for protection, for help crossing the road,
for justice in a traffic accident, and who call me at night
for a family quarrel . . .
the same people get at me for being a bully-boy, a Nazi.
They say I'm with 'Them' and against 'Us'; they
tell me I and my mates beat up prisoners,
arrest people simply to get another name and
promotion.
So, where am I, Lord?
I think I want to stick. I think I can do something to
help people who need help . . . so what I'm asking, Lord,
is 'Will you help me? Will you find me strength? Will you
help me, not to be a bent cop? Lord, I ask you, will you
help?'

YOU MUST BE JOKING, LORD

I'm empty

I'm empty; empty of love, of feeling and even of hate! I can't live in this vacuum. I've tried getting drunk, getting high on pot, but the emptiness returns and then everything seems even more useless.

I can't sleep

I cannot get off to sleep. Things, things — just things go round and round in my head. I cannot understand it, Lord. There is nothing really to worry me, but somehow I can't relax, I can't rest. I toss and turn in bed. Now and then I try reading, but it often doesn't work. I have tried counting sheep and praying . . . all sorts of things, but nothing seems to do any good. Give me peace, Lord, quiet me, help me to sleep. Amen.

Things that go bump in the night

Lord, I am afraid, there are so many noises in this dark night. Things crackle, go bump and there is a strange whispering. Lord, are you with me for I am fearful and alone, and dare not shut my eyes? Is there somebody walking about downstairs? Lord, calm me and make me realize that whatever happens nothing can separate me from you, not even the noises in the night, or even if someone coshes me. Reassure me of this and give me faith that your love will never let me go.

Seeing a dead person

Lord, I've just seen a dead person! At first I was shocked and didn't want to look at it, and then I wasn't afraid anymore. It's like looking at an empty house once lived in by somebody I've loved. It's dreadfully sad and yet somehow there is tremendous hope. The living spirit which made this rigid body something marvellous must be with you — what else could happen?

Somehow now death seems a little less frightening. Keep helping me to hope and trust so I shall not be so afraid of the thought of death.

Fire

I'm terrified of fire, Lord. When I go to bed at night or go out shopping, I turn everything off, and then five minutes after I want to go and check again that I really did turn off the gas. I always feel I'll wake to find flames all over the place, and sometimes I think I smell burning. It's a horrid feeling, Lord, and I ask you for two things. Help me to trust in you, calming my fears. And please keep me safe from fire tonight. Amen.

The dog scares me

The dog down the road, Lord, scares me each time I have to go by. It rushes out barking and snapping at my legs. Once or twice it has leapt right up at me and almost knocked me down. I really want to go round another way, but there is no other way. I've just got to be brave, only I'm not. So give me courage as I go to the shops this morning please, Lord.

Facing another week

Lord God, another week is beginning. I don't know how to face it. There are so many things I feel are just round the corner waiting to pounce on me . . . things I haven't done, things I should have done, things I've done and shouldn't. What a lot and what a little! But, will you see me through this week? It would not be fair to say: 'make it easy for me', because I don't deserve it, for what I've not done and done wrong. So, you see where I stand, Lord . . . I'm at the beginning of the week; I'm not sure: in fact I'm scared. So help me to face up and live through . . . I can't in honesty ask for any more. Amen.

This bike

See, Lord, there's this bike. I had my eye on it, and it's a beaut! Now, I've got it, it's all mine, except for the never-never, which goes on for two years. Only, I can't think of anything else.

It's great, Lord, great. And when I'm on it, I'm the greatest. It makes me six foot high, I can beat the world. I'm real, I'm a man, not a boy, I'm really me. And I want to say thank you to you, Lord, because I prayed and prayed and prayed, and worked and saved.

My mates say I'm crazy to say thank you to you — they say I did it all myself, with work and overtime, saving and skimping. They say it wasn't you, Lord. But I know in a funny way, if you had not been about, and I did not have the chance to talk to you, however hard I had worked, I would have fallen down and failed.

I believe this, Lord, and that is why, I want to say 'Thank you' . . . and I mean it . . . Thank you, Lord.

I'm afraid of evil

Lord, I'm afraid of the power of evil! They laugh at me for this, but not so much now since there've been films about people being possessed. In the dark and at night I don't worry about being beaten up, but I'm terrified of coming across evil spirits, and the evil that lurks in the places where violent and wicked men have lived and hated. Sometimes I sense hate and fear so much that it almost seems to smother me! But I know that you can heal or destroy this kind of evil, if I ask for your help. I make the sign of the cross as a quick way of calling on you and your power to save me from evil. Always be with me to protect me and strengthen my faith in your power to save and heal, I ask this trusting in the life-giving cross of Christ and in the power of his glorious resurrection. Amen.

YOU MUST BE JOKING, LORD

Out of touch

Will you teach me, Lord, how I can make contact, be in touch, get to know? I'm not sure how to put it, because I don't really know how to be in touch with you. But what am I trying to say? Well, other people seem to be able to talk to each other, they open up without fear, they say what they are and what they do. I just curl up inside, Lord, and say nothing. Other people fall in love. I don't think that I have ever really known or loved anybody, and I haven't let anybody know me; I'm too private; I don't want to let them in on my secrets. I don't think anyone has ever loved me. So, you see Lord, I'm out of touch, and I do so want to communicate, to be 'one of the family', to be known and loved. Well, I suppose even saying this to you is a bit of a break through, so will you help me to continue and go further, open, listen, talk, learn, and love?

When I'm cross

Lord, I've snapped at him again and been impatient. It's because I'm so dreadfully tired; I wouldn't do it otherwise because I love him. Help me to remember that you were patient and loving when people wouldn't leave you alone when you were tired and wanted to be by yourself. I know tiredness isn't really an excuse for being cross, so please forgive me, and help me to do better next time.

I am depressed

Did you ever meet people burdened by depression when you were on earth? Was the man who was possessed by devils depressed like me? Some deep force which I don't want to let into me drags me down into a gulf of misery. A black cloud surrounds me. I can't escape. There is no way out and it seems hopeless. Was your darkness on the cross like this? Lift me out of the depths. Say 'peace be still' in such a way as to stop the blackness burying me. Lay your cool hand on my brow and say 'Be whole again'. Heal me Lord, cast out my fears, my devils, my darkness. Save me, Lord, save me!

I struggle wearily on

Sometimes people talk about you, Jesus, as though you
    were Superman,
never tiring,
never fed up,
never angry,
never 'shut off' from God.
Then I hear about your followers,
the holy men and women,
and people say the same about them,
until it is impossible to try to follow.
But you know, I was looking through the Scripture,
and I came across this bit in Paul:
I struggle wearily on . . .
He had the humility to tell the Colossians

71

that work for them was a struggle,
and that he was kept going
because of your irresistible driving.
Then I thought a bit more about you,
and I remembered a passage which I found in John,
where you were tired and you sat at a well . . .
After that it began to crowd in . . . ,
driving buyers and sellers from the temple,
turning on Peter and rebuking him,
telling them that you had piped
and they would not dance,
weeping . . . for Jerusalem . . . for Lazarus,
crying on the cross —
'Why hast thou forsaken me'.
So, now Lord, I can begin to admit
that I struggle wearily on.
Often I think: 'Is it worth it?'
Often I almost despair.
But then I can begin to think:
Jesus tired,
Jesus alone,
Jesus deserted,
Jesus weeping,
Jesus 'forsaken by God' . . .
And perhaps I begin to understand
what you asked when you said 'Follow me'.
I will try now to follow,
because I know you found it hard
and so I will find it hard . . . it is what you offered.
So be it.
Amen.

Knotted me

I'm all tied up. I know they are trying to help me. I want to be helped. But I hate being helped too. Part of me is kicking at them, sulking, turning the other way, refusing everything. And part of me is crying deep inside, wanting help, wanting love, in agony of need. But I'm too proud and too tied up to ask or even to accept. O Lord, I can ask you! Untie this knotted me.

Make me lovable

Lord make me lovable! No one seems to love me, Lord. How do I start being lovable? Help me, Lord, by loving me. If you love me, give me a sign of your concern, for then I shall be happier, and perhaps more attractive to others and they will love me. So show me your love, Lord.

Drunk

Lord, help, help! I know I've drunk too much. I wanted to forget and I did. Now I am so dizzy and swingy that I want to lie down. But if I lie down I feel as if I were dropping down a dark, deep well and I don't know where I'll end up. It is all so horrible that I won't ever drink so much again. It is better to put up with distress than this nightmare. Please make it end and let me sleep. Lord, forgive me!

Give me patience

O God give me patience. She's at it again! Nag, nag, nag! O God I know I'm at fault too, but God give me patience!

Excuses

Lord, I am always making excuses when I don't get things done, or when things go wrong. I often blame other people or tell a downright lie in case I'm found to be wrong and get told off. I don't know why I hate being told off so much; I suppose it wounds my self-love. It's odd because I know I've done wrong, but the excuses come out before I can stop them. Take me over so completely and enter into my life so fully that I will be unable to make excuses but will accept blame and tellings off, humbly if possible, or at least not looking sulky!

Pilfering

Lord, I don't know how to keep doing what I think is right. Where I work everyone pinches things; in a self-service store it is easy. They laugh at me when I say it's stealing and tell me that I should take things too as it is part of the perks. Lord, it's hard for Mum to feed the family with prices going up and up and it would be easy for me to take things from time to time; no-one would notice. Give me the courage, Lord, to keep on refusing to steal however much I'm tempted, for it is very hard to be honest in a permissive world!

Violence

Lord, I've just got caught in this demo! I can't get out and they're getting violent. Stay with me; stop me from being infected by the violence, and from hitting, kicking, and pushing like the rest! Give me courage and the right kind of strength. Amen.

I'm just existing

A dull, grey/white cottonwool surrounds me, Lord. It isn't light; it isn't dark; it isn't something I can touch; it isn't real and makes everything else unreal — you, the world, my family, my home, my job — life itself. I beat on the grey/white cottonwool, but it is still all round me. Please, Lord, send a ray of your light to pierce through this cottonwool, so that I may live, not just exist.

I forgot!

Lord, I've forgotten to keep that date! It was dreadfully important. What will they say? What can I do now? Can I tell the truth and say I forgot? Should I make untrue excuses because they won't trust me again if they knew I just forgot? Lord, make them understand, and give me courage to do the right thing!

Tempted to steal

Lord, it would be so easy to take just a little money from her purse. I've none at all and there are so many things I need. She'd never be quite sure the money had gone. I do need so many things, don't I Lord? Yet I suppose taking just a little money is stealing — O Lord take this temptation away for I'm sure it is wrong to steal however great my need. Amen.

On the motorway

Lord, keep me safe on the motorway. Keep me awake and stop me from doing anything that will be dangerous for others as well as myself. It is easy to forget to look in the mirror before going out into the fast lane — don't let me do this. I get fussed by lorries which come up so close to me that I can't see whether it is safe to go into another lane; so help me to keep calm and patient whatever happens. Don't let me get annoyed so that I go fast just to show off and pay them off for crowding me.

Protect me from the carelessness of others and from driving carelessly myself.

I'm fed up with elections!

We are always having elections, Lord. When it isn't a general one it's one for the local council. I don't know where they get us. I know most of us are fed up with them and with politicians. I wonder if you were political, Jesus? Some say you were, and I can see it is a way to try to get things done. But I wonder too whether you would have spent all this time that we pay people to sit on committees making plans which lead to more committees which make more plans. I think with you something would have happened. But how could I, Lord, do anything which would make a difference? I'd gladly try, but I get fed up and can't see the point. If there is a way for me, please show me, Lord.

I never married

Lord, I'm still single, unmarried. Somehow it never happened. I always wanted to be married, but often in a vague kind of way, and it just passed me by. Now I'm getting older and all my friends and relations have their children and their homes, and I am so very much alone. I get jealous and full of self-pity. It's too late: I know I'll never marry, but Lord, I feel unfulfilled, unused — yes, unloved, Lord. So, give me courage not to go into a depression, interest to be active for others, love to cut out jealousy, and something which will make me know my life is not entirely useless. I'm sorry, Lord, this is a very selfish prayer . . . but you know me and know how I'm placed . . . so have mercy on me, Lord.

YOU MUST BE JOKING, LORD

Crisis

The whole of your world, Lord, is caught in crisis. I am not talking of war. You know there is enough of that! I mean what they call economics. I mean that we are caught between the people who are starving, the people who are homeless, the people who suffer disease, disintegration and despair . . . and the people who have 'enough', and the people who have 'more than enough' and the people who have too much. Now, I only think I have enough, and not really enough for what I want. But can you do two things, Lord. Can you teach me how I stand — do I really only have enough, or is it 'too much' in your sense? And can you make the same thing clear, whatever you may say, to the tycoons who control these things? I'm in a muddle, Lord. I think a lot of others are too. Will you straighten us out?

This job

Lord, help me to get this job. I want it more than anything else I've ever asked you for. It's interesting, exciting and just what I want. There will be a lot of people after it, but please Lord, let me get it! If I did I'd do my best to make a real go of it, so do help me, Lord. Amen.

HIM, HER, IT

'All animals are equal, but some are more equal than others.' George Orwell's phrase is so well known that it is hackneyed.

Let us use it as a starting place for a thought.

The kind of animals we are thinking about (and so was Orwell in story form) are mostly human, but we do not want to exclude any creature, because the very word 'creature' implies the One behind creation.

In our prayer, whether we are in joy or doubt or hatred, we may come to this state because of a 'thing'. Stub your toe against a chair leg, marvel at the beauty of a sunset, be put into doubt about God's goodness by a devastating earthquake. Well, each of these comes into the 'It' category . . . and there are many more 'Its' in our lives. What are yours?

For some of us, animals (cats, dogs, birds and so on) are just animals, a series of 'Its'. But for others they become 'persons', with names and characteristics, 'personalities', you might say. This may seem strange, to those who do not understand, but it is true.

And the funny thing which can happen with many people is that they come to treat the mass or the individual human being more like a less considered animal, or even like an 'It' . . . a case, a pawn, an object. Is the 'policeman' allowed a personality? Is the 'doctor' real? Does the priest or the minister have more than a cardboard image, not even carrying a proper name?

Only knowledge basically leads to allowing 'Him' or 'Her' a full personality . . . knowledge leading on to trust, understanding and love. It is too easy for us to let the generality of mankind remain in the 'It' stage, whereas the Christian really following Christ must learn to treat each and every individual as real, a son of God, and one to be respected, known and loved.

The prayers that follow are for Him, Her, and It.

We hope they reflect the problem and the possibility of the richness which God has lavished on the world — for it — the world itself — is worthy of more attention and care than we would often give it.

And once we have come to that point, we may recall that Jesus told us that his Father and ours has numbered every hair on our heads, knows when every sparrow falls, and cares individually for us who are of little faith.

So what can our response be to each creation of such a loving God other than interest, understanding and love?

SHORT PRAYERS

He'll kill himself, if he goes on like that. Save him, Lord.

Lord, make him care a little and need me a little!

He's shallow and he has an important job to do. Deepen him, Lord!

I hate everything about my job, and I can't get out of it. What can I do, Lord?

Please don't let him get sent down. I love him, Lord.

Lord, strengthen her; she is in such pain.

She's given herself to him, Lord, and he's not fit for her. She'll be hurt by him: he'll break her heart. Soften the pain, Lord.

He drinks too much. He's crashed his car and smashed his face. Give him courage now.

It's so cruel and so crazy, Lord. How can I love your cross?

God forgive me. I wish she were dead.

God bless her. She is the most wonderful woman in the world.

The way she bears that terrible pain is most moving, Lord. Give her courage, give her strength, give her a little respite, Lord.

It doesn't make sense. It's plain stupid to me, but your will be done, Lord.

So . . . it's another war and more killing! Why can't it be peace?

The wonder of love! It's good to be loved. Send more of it through your world, Lord.

Such a tiny thing. How beautiful and fragile and perfect she is. Thank you for letting me share in making her, Lord.

The swallow has built a nest outside my window. I thank you for it, Lord.

It's raining hard; the bus is late. Make it come soon, please, Lord.

What a wonderful thing that a dog can be trained to lead and help the blind. Your creation is wonderful, Lord.

She says she believes nothing. Lord, show her the way. I don't seem to be able to do so.

Please stop him from talking the whole time! It's driving me mad!

Peace is so far away. Bring it closer to our hearts, Lord.

Moonlight shatters my wakefulness, covers the world in icy beauty. Lord, melt the ice, and leave the beauty.

Mum fusses

Lord, did your mother fuss? Mine does like mad: I'm
sure yours didn't if she's like what we are told about her.
Yet I remember she was upset when you went off to the
temple on your own. I hope she did fuss a bit and then
you'll understand how I feel! It helps when I know that
you had to put up with the sort of things we have to
and that you didn't shout at her to shut up the way I do.
I don't want to shout really but I get fed up with her
fussing. Show me how to stay calm and to soothe her
down so I can tell her that I know what I'm up to, and
know how to look after myself. This would be such a
help, Lord.

My baby

Lord, I do thank you so much for our baby. She is
lovely even if she looks a bit wizened and old when she
puckers up her face. But I wish you had given me more
knowledge of babies. I get so worried at night that I get
out of bed to see if she is really breathing. I know it's
silly but I get anxious when there is no sound from the
cot. Help me to learn how to look after her, and give me
more trust in you who protect us both. Make me peaceful
and calm in all my dealings with her now and throughout
her life.

Why do I hurt my baby?

Lord, why do you let me bang my baby about? I love

83

her so much. She is all I have. And I want her to love me
and she doesn't! She wouldn't scream and cry so much
if she did.

Joe's at work, the pub, the dogs, rarely at home, and
when he is he swears and hits me. Then she yells and
yells, and 'cause I'm cornered and hurt, I thump her
because she doesn't love me either. Why won't someone
love me? Mum hates me, always has, and now my baby
is beginning to as well. Somehow, stop me for getting
mad with this hateful world, and with her — please Lord,
if you do really love little children as they say you do!

Jealous of him

Lord, I am jealous! A friend of mine says it's a low
grade sin, but it seems natural if you love someone to
worry in case he finds someone else more attractive and
interesting. When I see him talking and laughing with
other girls, I want to rush up and tell him to come away.
He hates me if I do this and says I don't trust him. Well,
I don't! Take this gnawing jealousy out of my heart,
Lord. It makes both him and me miserable, but somehow
it takes hold of me and I can't get out of its clutches.
Show me how to love trustingly without being possessive.
Give me love like yours. You are forgiving and take us
back even though we keep rushing after so many other
gods besides you. Stop me from being jealous I beg
you, Lord!

He doesn't love me now!

Lord, he said he loved me and would never leave me, and I really believed him! Now he says his feelings have 'changed'. I love him with all my being and, without him, life seems empty. For so long I have lived each day thinking of the next time we'd meet and the joy of the thought of it coloured all my living. Now all is blackness and greyness, and there seems to be no future. I can't even hate. Lord, thaw me out; help me to feel and live again. I will never be able to trust a man again. Nothing seems sure and fixed any more. This lack of security is numbing. Be a support and a rock for me to cling to in my dark world, and, in time, give me the ability to trust and to love again, for you, I know, will never desert me.

He treats me like a stranger

Lord, we've quarrelled and I'm utterly miserable. I don't know what to do! He treats me like a stranger; whatever I do or say makes no difference. When I try to be amusing, he just looks at me coldly. I've tried to apologise but he does not respond, not even to tell me that it was my fault! I am frozen inside and weary, and without any idea what to do now. I love him so much and it hurts. Lord, I love you too; don't leave me, but give me your peace so I can keep going and break this deadlock in our lives. Amen.

YOU MUST BE JOKING, LORD

Rain

I was walking in the rain, Lord;
it's always raining here.
Sometimes it makes me so depressed I want
to weep.
But today, Lord, it was a luminous rain, which
shone in the puddles and on passing cars;
it splashed off gutters and slooshed down the streets.
It was good, Lord, and I walked and sang
in the rain.
How easy it is to complain in gloomy skies and
dark days, when all the earth frowns,
and my soul weeps.
But how beautiful is rain, soft or driving,
bringing life, with all things fresh and new —
even the dingy old factories and dwellings — shining
in a later ray of sun . . .
then shoot and sprout between the broken paving stones
shaking a glistening drop, the yellow crossing lights
reflecting black and white across the road . . .
and all because of you and your thought for man.
Alleluia, Lord, God of the elements, maker of rain. Amen.

Her

My heart raced, when I saw her, Lord. She's perfect,
and I so much want to know her, Lord. Please make it
possible, and if we do meet Lord, please make us click!

The pop-star

This pop-star, he turns me on, Lord. Is this wrong? When we go to hear him, he just gets us! I get caught all of me, by his singing, by his slinky, shiney white suit, by the rhythm of his jungle kind of walk. We scream and shout for him, for more. Is this wrong, Lord; is a jungle kind of experience wrong? I just don't know! Is he becoming, in our lives, what you should be to us? Should you turn us on, Lord? So often your priests, and ministers, and churchy people just turn me off — I think they and you should turn me on. Am I wrong, Lord?

Forgiving

Oh God! How many more times? Seventy times seven you said? Well then, give me strength, please!

Help her to forgive

Someone she had worked for turned on her, Lord, and got her sent to prison. Help her to forgive the wrong she was done; help the wrong doer to see her own guilt. And please let us respect other people and as Jesus said 'turn the other cheek'.

A quiet person

Tonight I met a quiet person who spoke to me of your love, Lord. Thank you.

YOU MUST BE JOKING, LORD

Make her love me

I thought it was going quite well tonight, Lord,
at the dance, I mean. She was friendly
and we talked, we laughed, we had a drink
together and we danced again, and again.
Then, the end came, and we walked home
together — I mean, I saw her home, Lord —
I wasn't staying with her.
But on the way she went silent, and we
walked in silence, and we walked in silence,
and we walked in silence.
Nothing! I tried a sentence — no reply;
I tried a question — only a grunt.
When we parted at her door, we did not kiss.
What have I done, Lord? She would not say.
Is it just natural and passing, or is it real
and final?
I don't know, Lord. I'm just
waiting to see, because there is nothing else to
do — and the waiting
is worse than the ending — yet is it, Lord?
I cannot judge. My parents say there are other girls,
and that I know. But only this ONE girl!
I want her, Lord, but I do not understand her. Will
you guide me, help me? And is there anything
you can say to her about me which will help?
I hope so, Lord!
Because I'm confused now; I don't
know what I've done wrong, or what she wants,
But I love her Lord, so put in a word for me,
or put words in my mouth. Oh, Lord, I love her!

Stop my father from telling her what to do

Lord, please stop Dad from telling her what we should do, where we should live, and from trying to organise our lives. She won't say what she thinks of him and his views to his face, but, Lord, I'll hear about it for weeks after! I love my father and my wife, but why can't they try to understand each other? They won't make the smallest effort to understand each other as far as I can see. They both know what they want for me is the right thing! Help me to know how to set about getting them to be open-minded, or at least a little open-minded about each other. Lord, work in their hearts and make them more loving and give me strength to stop shouting at them and making a scene. So stop Dad from telling her what to do!

Must I go back to him?

Lord, how can I go back to him? Is it my duty? His nagging and jealousy makes me go into myself and become all tensed up. This gets into the baby too and she whines and whimpers. It isn't good for us at all! but she blossoms and smiles, and chortles when he and I are apart and I am relaxed and not on guard the whole time; yet a child needs a father! I don't know what to do for the best. Perhaps if I loved you more deeply and felt secure in your love, I would not curl up when he was jealous and difficult; perhaps then he'd grow to trust me and love me in a less possessive way. You said all things

were possible if we have faith, so please increase my faith.
Amen.

I'm torn between you and him

Lord, you seemed to call me. It took a long time,
but in the end, I answered you. I accepted Christianity,
I even joined your church. In a way, I knew it would
not be easy.
But, Lord, I didn't know my husband would react
like this.
I only have to mention church, or those I've met there,
and he just switches off.
On Sundays I go off to church, come back and carry
    on . . .
Silence! It is as though that ninety minutes of walk and
church never happened.
So what do I do, Lord? Give in and let him ride me,
against my conscience and my desire,
because he married me, and this is top priority?
Or do I cut loose a little, go to meetings,
talk of you to others, come alive?
I'm torn, Lord, because there are two sides to my life.
You, and then him and the family.
I'm in a muddle, I'm torn, I just don't know which way
to go.
So now, having thought and thought, I'm handing it
to you, Lord.
If there is an answer, help me find it, if not —
so be it, Lord.

Fed up with my child

Lord, life if ghastly and I don't know what to do.
My child is with me all day long, needing watching and
listening to non-stop! She opens cupboards, takes things
out, pulls things off the table and is never still all day.
I never get a let-up. I love her but she nearly drives me
mad! If I knew anyone in this town it would be easier,
but I am alone here all day with no one to talk to and
never a moment to read. When my husband comes in I'm
tired and grumpy and no fun for him. It seems so hopeless.
Show me what to do; give me the energy to try and
meet people. Or send someone to visit me. Give me
some hope – show me somehow that this won't go on
for ever, and make my husband more understanding!
Help me, Lord.

Her only child has been killed

She was knocked down on the pedestrian crossing.
She died in hospital with her mother beside her. The
grief of this widowed mother losing her only child is
awful, Lord. Have mercy on her.

Driving test

Lord, you may think it is silly of me to ask about such
a thing, but could you help me to pass my driving test?
I've learnt the Highway Code and have done everything

I should so as to be able to pass, but I am not always as good at backing round corners as I should be though mostly I get it right. So please make me have a good day and do everything correctly! Amen.

House-keeping accounts and him

Lord, help, help, I've messed up my house-keeping accounts again — they just won't balance! He'll go on and on about writing down the cost of the things that I buy, and about my extravagance. I don't mean it to be like this; it just seems to happen! I'll weep and he'll storm. Keep me calm, patient and loving and able to explain that I don't mean the accounts to go wrong and that I just forget to do things. Please help me to be more organised, though I haven't much hope about this! Perhaps you could help me to keep trying to improve!

My dog has been run over

Lord, I'm going mad! My dog has been run over. He's dead. Oh God, I loved him so much. Why did it happen?

My cat

Lord, I find it much easier to love my cat than my mother; give me balance, Lord.

Battered wife

It's terrible, Lord,
if there's Hell . . . then this is it!
I only married him a few weeks ago . . . he
was all I wanted for a boy and the father of
our children.
But, Lord, the day he married me, it
all changed. I'd been out with him for
months before the wedding. We talked of everything,
we even gave names to the children we would have,
we lived and laughed and planned and saved . . .
and we were married in church.
That night, Lord, he beat me up . . . I could not believe
    it!
He said he loved me, and hit me across the face!
O Lord, since then it's been going on and on and on.
Each night I cry myself to sleep and he snores beside
me. Worn out? Satisfied? Happy? O Lord!
So what am I to do, Lord? I'm only twenty-two.
I don't think Mum will have me back. She's
got a new boy friend since Dad died.
And, I'm pregnant, Lord. He may hurt my baby, if I
stay with him; but what will I do, if I leave
him?
Oh, help me, Lord . . . stop him beating me up or
give me courage to go . . . I'm dithering and
I cannot decide, I cannot sit still, I can't even
pray . . . Oh help me, Lord!

Hatred of him

From the very bottom of my whole being there comes a great hatred, Lord. I know you tell me to love my enemy, but how can I when he keeps on persecuting, needling, bugging me? Can't you stop him, because I want to love not hate, and hate is all that grows in my heart for him. I know it's wrong, I know I should forgive, and, God help me, I just hate more deeply. I feel completely lost and unable to change. If you don't do something, then the hell I'm suffering looks like lasting now and for ever. Have mercy on me, Lord.

The baby's crying

Lord, the child's crying again and I'll have to get out of bed into the cold to see to her! Why can't her father get up for once? It isn't fair that I have to do it every time! It's enough to make me join women's lib. Help me not to resent being a woman, and stop me from going on at my husband for not getting up. Even though it's the middle of the night, keep me loving, Lord.

Lord, the baby is crying and I'll have to get up again, couldn't you make him sleep longer? I'm getting so tired, and I get scratchy and difficult to live with when I have so little sleep. Lord please teach me to do the right things to encourage him to sleep, and make him more restful and not so demanding. I can't think why you have given me such a restless baby. Give him and me more peace!

Laughing in Church

I couldn't help laughing in church today, Lord. There was this woman and her hat. I couldn't help thinking she looked like a cod with a bit of seaweed caught in its fins. Sorry, Lord, but you do make us laughable, and I hope you see the joke, Lord, because I think sometimes we need to laugh in church or else it's all too unreal.

Make me patient with Gran

Lord, give me patience with Gran, who when there are others around will show off and say loudly what happened to her in the past and talk about her illnesses and interrupt our conversations. She is just like a small child who wants attention! What she says is often boring and I feel ashamed for her. Forgive me, Lord, and stop me from shutting her up, and if possible make her more interested in us and our problems. Make us all more understanding and loving in a sensible kind of way!

I can't understand my child

Lord, help me. I just can't understand my child! He is as shut up as a clam and does not react to anything I say. Show me how to get through this barrier he puts round himself. If I have done or said something that has made him close up, let me know what it is, so I can explain myself. Lord, give me a spirit of discernment and understanding; make me more open to you and to him. Let him see that I love him and want to be loved back!

YOU MUST BE JOKING, LORD

She's bossy

My mother's very bossy — always telling me to get on with things when I want just to be sitting thinking, reading, or wondering about things. Perhaps the things I think about seem silly to her, but they are important to me. I like to look at the sea, the trees, the sky, and watch the shapes of the clouds and wonder why they change as they move along, and things like that! She thinks I should be going walks, playing games, rushing about with others or doing shopping for her when I'm not at school work. She keeps on at me in a bossy way. I'm sure your mother was peaceful to live with and allowed you to sit quietly when you wanted to, and that she was loving in an understanding way and didn't try to make you into the kind of person she wanted. I'm sure she was restful to be with. Dad says mine can't rest or let others rest. Could you help her to be quieter and let Dad and I have a rest from being bossed?

Seeing the boss

Lord, I'm scared; my tummy is all churned up! I've got to see the boss and I'm not sure why! I don't think I've done wrong. Stop me from looking frightened, because then I'll look as if I'm guilty. Keep me calm; keep saying to me 'peace be still' so I'll be able to think what I'm saying if she questions me. Make her understanding, and calm me, Lord. Amen.

My Mum wants me to go to church

Lord, I am struggling to find out for myself if you do exist. I can't go to communion if I don't believe in you. It just wouldn't be honest, and I have to be honest when I am trying to find out what life is about. Then Dad and Mum nag me and say I must go to church, and say that it looks funny if I don't and the young ones will get put off and not go either. I'd like to please Mum, but the nagging only makes me see how important it is that I should work it out for myself so that it can become real and meaningful for me, and not just something I do to please them. Make them see that they must leave me to have it out with you, and that I can't believe just because they tell me to. I want to understand and believe, so give me courage to search honestly!

She wants me to pray with her

I don't know what I'm to do. I don't believe you exist, but Jane wants me to talk to you with her before she goes to bed! At school they pray. And it seems to be something she wants to do and likes to do. She talks to you the way she talks to me and has no doubt that you are about and care for her. What she does is honest, but what about me? When I don't believe there is a you? It seems mad, but because she is so sure I'm shaken, so help me if you are there!

YOU MUST BE JOKING, LORD

Her first day at school

Lord, I'm worried, it's her first day at school. She seems so little to go off on her own and she is so used to everyone being loving and kind to her. I am afraid that she will get hurt and lose her self-confidence. I know I can't protect her all her life, and I must trust that the warmth and love she gets at home will help to strengthen her. I know she will meet with rebuffs, for children can be so truthfully unkind to each other, but Lord, keep her from being embittered by the small hurts, the mockings which will probably seem so enormous to her. Show her how to grow and develop through the upsets in her life and help me to know how to encourage her. Help me to teach her how to trust and rely on you in her distress and to thank you for the good things in her life.

Make her lovable

If you want me to love her, Lord, can you, please, make her lovable? Or teach me how to love the unlovable!

Mum's problem

My Mum is at the end of her tether; she just can't cope with the children, and I can't help a lot as I'm away at work all day. Now she's expecting another baby, and she's neglecting the others already! They are always in trouble with the police and she can't control them, but yells and screams at them so they act worse. I'm scared she'll go off her head if she has another child. She knows that some of my friends have had abortions and is wondering about one herself. What can we do,

Lord? If she goes mad or cracks up what will happen to the children? We don't think abortion's right, but is it right to have a child that is neglected? I'm afraid they'll all end up in borstal and prison. What is the right and loving solution? All solutions seem horrific! What should she do, Lord?

Dependent on him

Lord, it's hard! When I was out at work I'd my own money to buy what I wanted. But now I'm dependent on him. I never know whether he'll give me money for a dress, or whether he'll look after the baby so I can go to a meeting in the evening. It's all so uncertain, and I can't plan at all. How do I talk to him, Lord, so that we reach some sort of agreement so I'll know where I am and not completely dependent on his whims? You'd think if he loves me as he says he does, he'd want me to be happy and not unsettled. It's enough to make a woman join women's lib! Stop me from being aggressive and make him a bit more understanding!

He's hurt me

He has hurt me so much that I long to wound him too. Then, Lord, I think that if I do this I might undermine his self-confidence, so I don't do it. But most of all I know that hitting back to hurt is against your law of love, and this, even more than any other reason, stops me from doing it. It is utterly unfair that you take from us our human weapons and leave us defenceless to bear the pain others inflict. It's your fault

I am so miserable and defenceless, so it is up to you to comfort and sustain me. So please start now, and why did you give me a fighting spirit that wants to hit back?

I want my child baptised

I went to see this vicar, Lord. And he said I couldn't get my child baptised. I didn't see why, but he said did I ever go to church? Well, I said sometimes which means when I was christened and when my Nan was buried . . . Oh, and when our Jim married his bit from Leeds (or was it Liverpool? I can't remember, Lord, but they're in the First Division). Anyhow, he said I couldn't and I don't see what right he has to stop me having my Sally baptised. After all, you made her really, Lord. I know John and I did it together, but you are the creator, Lord, and in a way we both agree about you, and we did say a prayer the day the Clinic said I was pregnant. We said; 'Thank you, Lord!' Do you remember? Anyhow, as I was saying, I don't see what right he has. And you know, if he won't do it, I think I'll do it myself. After all, Lord, you said you came for sinners . . . and that's us!
. . . so why should your vicar be so snooty? . . . Oh, yes, I know what you will say Lord, about doing things the proper way . . . but I wonder if you did Lord, as Jesus Christ, when you broke the rules and went ahead because a person needed you . . . if an ox or an ass falls in the pit on the Sabbath day, you said, would you leave it there or get it out, law or no law? That's what you asked . . . And now I just say to you; 'Teach me to see, and teach your vicar to see, and then perhaps you will bring us together so that we both see . . . Please, Lord!

US/WE

There was an old man once who worked as a caddie at a golf club. When he spoke to the player he was assisting he always used the terms 'Us' and 'We'. 'Us will use a No. 2 here, we will'. He came to be known as 'Us and We' by everyone.

There are some things we do alone. But very many things we do with one or more other people. Indeed, it could be argued that we never do anything alone, except perhaps die, because there is a great, interwoven support system in creation. From the moment of conception we are community people.

Some of us choose later to be more alone; some are alone with loneliness, somehow cut off or unable to make relationships.

But relationship is the very stuff of life. Even a person alone will commune with nature or with God. And most people will naturally relate.

However, the weight of the teaching of Christ, drawn from the Law and the Prophets and developed by him, is on man accepting a 'WE nature' and a 'WE religion'.

Because 'I' am always there in the relationship, and 'I' is so close to and important to 'ME', some training, discipline and generosity is essential if we are to grow.

In this section, we pick out some relationships. They are only pointers to the wonderfully complex and simple pattern which makes up human living. The hope we have is that such prayers as are here will lead you on, individually and together, to express, widen and deepen the 'Us and We' in God's world.

SHORT PRAYERS

Alone we can do nothing, Lord. With you, we can do all.

Keep us, guard us, watch us, save us, Lord.

We are yours, we are yours. Thank you, Lord, that we are yours!

Turn our hearts of stone to hearts of flesh. Give us feeling, Lord.

Show us how to live in peace. Teach us how to stop fighting, Lord.

Why must we be battered and hurt in order to become real, Lord?

Why, if we want peace in the world, do we do so little about it, Lord?

What's got into us, Lord? We used to be so close. Now we are always getting at each other — unite us again!

We make idols

Lord, people say the ten commandments are out of date, but are they? They say we don't make idols and worship them instead of you. But it seems to me your place in our lives gets taken by things — things like a colour T.V., a new car, a super motor bike, or even trendy clothes! We think so much about them, or want to own them if we don't have them, that they become the chief things in our lives. When we should be thinking of you, and loving you and others, we are thinking of them and almost fall in love with them! Stop us from becoming slaves to things that have no lasting value. Make us see that nothing can take your place in our lives without damaging us, and give us grace to know you better.

It's wonderful being married

Lord, it's wonderful being married and we do thank you for the joy of it. We haven't much furniture and the flat needs decorating badly, but it is an adventure doing things together so as to make it look nicer. We may never have much money, but we have each other. This is wonderful. Help us always to be loving and able to share things. Whatever happens help us to remember that you are with us in our love, and will help us with all our problems.

YOU MUST BE JOKING, LORD

We're superficial

Lord, it's easy today to live on a surface level, and never go deeply into anything. So much work is mechanical and we don't need to apply our minds to it, and somehow we jog along not thinking of anything very much. The newspapers give little snippets of information, the T.V. and radio do the same, so we don't need to think very much except about keeping amused and superficially occupied. Did you create us for such a shallow way of living? I can see us becoming mindless objects not fearing or loving deeply at all! Help us to get out of this self-living before it is too late, and show us how to enjoy life and to live on more than one dimension. Lift us out of this superficiality and show us how to live fully, Lord!

Sorry for us

I stopped suddenly in the street the other day, Lord. I had been hurrying along, a little late for work, and everyone else was hurrying too. It hit me then . . . why am I hurrying? Where am I going? Where are they all going?

And it seemed to me that I was going off to produce a bit of machinery which is really only a luxury. We could all do without it. Yet I am making it day in and day out. The adverts say every hosue should have one!

But why Lord, when so many are starving? Why waste energy when it is running out? Why try to make and sell something we could well do without, and in the 'sacrifice' involved, do something really worth while, like feeding the hungry or clothing the naked.

Were we all born for this, Lord, or has someone led us down a cul-de-sac of greed and frustration? Lord show us the true values, teach us how to live. Open our eyes to see our common need hidden under our common greed. Amen.

We live in my mother-in-law's house

Lord, we are going round the bend living in my in-laws' house. We've only this one room to ourselves, and we have to cook together, watch the T.V. with them and we're never alone much. She is always telling me what to do and how to do it. She takes his side against me, and then we quarrel and shout at each other, and though I still love him it is getting harder and harder to keep loving. Lord, help us to find a flat somewhere else so that we could be together and get to know each other without interference the whole time. Lord, if you feel strongly about divorce, why don't you do something to help us before it's too late!

We quarrel about the telly

Lord, we quarrel about the telly in a most dreadful way! We swear at each other when we don't get the programmes we want. It's horrible! What can we do about it? It's ruining our family life! Dad likes westerns, no-one else does; Mum hates 'top of the pops' and says she can't get away from the noise in our tiny house. It's hell when we all want different programmes. It means someone is always banging about, or sulking and spoiling it for the others. What can we do? Draw lots, take turns? Help us to be nice to each other when we don't get what we want, and make us more reasonable and less heated about it, Lord, because except for the telly, I think we are a loving family!

Family quarrel

They've been at it again, Lord. Generally they wait till I'm in bed, but sometimes they go off against each other when I'm there. Can't you stop them Lord? You know I love them both, Mum and Dad, but sometimes she is all uptight and then he goes out and has a drink, and she lets him have it when he comes back and he shouts at her, and says he's leaving. Lord, don't let him go, but do something to them. Let them see we all love them and want them both, not just one; and we want them thinking of us, and not fighting each other. And we want the peace and fun the family used to have, with Mum cooking and Dad taking us to football on a Saturday. So, Lord, I'll try to get the others to ask you, and try to keep Mum and Dad from parting, but there's an awful lot for you to do too, Lord. Please will you?

Our prayer and yours

Help us to remember, Lord, that the prayer you
gave us is a family prayer. It's an 'our' prayer and not a
'my' prayer and it stays this way even if we say it alone.
Help us to pray it remembering that we belong to the
family of man, and that we adore you, confess our sins,
ask forgiveness, pray for daily needs and deliverance
from evil on behalf of the whole of sinful mankind, and
not just for ourselves. You are our Father, Lord, and we
thank you for this and for our relationships with others.
Amen.

We can't be instant Christians

Lord, today everything's instant! There's instant
coffee, instant tea, instant meals, instant love-making.
We expect everything to happen instantly without any
waiting! But, Lord, I find there isn't an instant foot-
baller, rarely an instant scientist; some things need
working at, and there isn't an instant Christian! We try
to get close to you, to be intimate with you by taking
drugs, by developing techniques, but it doesn't work!
You, through your Spirit can give us instant glimpses of
you, but then you leave us, so we come to realise that
we have to work and plod at getting to know you, and
you, with infinite patience mould us, sculpt us into the
kind of person you would like us to be. There are so
many casualties of instant living in our world, so please
mould us gently, smooth our roughness, and help us to

107

keep turning ourselves to you peacefully and calmly so that we can come to know you more deeply.

Black and white love

We are going along together, walking, talking, loving a little. It is all very wonderful, our growing love. There is only one snag, and that is I am black and she is white. Oh, I don't see it as a snag, nor does she, but both lots of parents do. She has hers refusing to let me come in the house; my old man just curses when he sees me with her. I suppose they're intolerant, but so are some of my mates. We talk about it together, she and I, and we think, Lord, it is our problem and not their business. They say what about our children. I don't know, Lord, but surely we can work that out? If we love each other and the children, can't we go ahead? Oh, I know there will be difficulties, but we'll keep praying, Lord, and trying to do the right thing. So, help us please, and if it isn't right to go ahead, then open our eyes to the danger and give us the courage for what we must do.

Why are we so self-centred?

Lord, why are we so self-centred when we surely see what a mess self-centredness makes of lives and countries? Men grabbing things for themselves, for their own group, make the weaker people lose out and suffer. Each of us is guilty; though you told us to deny ourselves, we only indulge ourselves. Lord help us to break the bondage of our selfishness, and let us really know, and not just say we do, what it means to deny ourselves. Stop us from buying and hoarding things we don't need now in case the economic situation gets worse. The temptation to hoard, to try to buy security, is very great and real, even if it is bought at the expense of others. Lord, save us from our selfishness!

We pray together

We sometimes pray together, Lord, because it is so wonderful to be in love. And so we pray this one today.

We want to tell you from the bottom of our hearts how wonderful it is to be alive, how wonderful it is to love each other, and how, for us, this came through you. The truth is that we both prayed to you and trusted you. We both wanted to fall in love and marry, but it had not happened for us.

But then, Lord, it happened. I suppose anyone could call it chance. We just met at a party, and suddenly . . . it blew . . . we fell in love – bang.

Only just before we married, we were talking one night and somehow both of us realised for the first time that we had been praying; that you were involved, and we felt terrific.

So now we are married and are settling together, we

wanted just to tell you this and say 'Thank you', because it is so wonderful to be in love. Keep us that way, Lord, please.

Help us to see the funny side

Lord, I've been reading that people who are devoted to extreme left- or right-wing causes are without humour. Somehow their devotion doesn't allow them to relax, look at themselves and the world and laugh; they are constantly serious! Lord, this can easily happen to your followers. This is ridiculous, for loving you should bring us joy and the ability to see the funny side of life. You told us the story of the man who had such a large plank in his eye that he couldn't see to take the speck of dust out of his friend's eye! We read this with great seriousness and can't realise what a comic picture it is! Then there is the camel trying to get through the eye of a needle! I don't know but it seems to me we are too serious about ourselves, and not full of the self-forgiving joy which you offer us. So do help us to laugh more, and particularly at ourselves, Lord!

Our selfishness

Let your Spirit blow Lord; your beautiful earth is covered with the cobwebs of our selfishness.

Forgive us

You gave us the world to look after, to cultivate and to bring to flower and fruit. Look how we rape it in our greed, Lord. Forgive us and teach us to care for your creation.

Give us peace

Lord, perhaps above all things today we need the gift of peace. We are anxious about so many things. We worry about our standard of living, about what people think of us, whether we can keep up the pace of life, whether we have an identity. Anxiety drives so many people out of their minds. Save us from anxiety; show us how to accept that your love for us is real and that nothing can separate us from it; give us that interior peace which is untouched by the outer storms of life. When we get excited, worried, anxious, say to us calmly, quietly as you did to the waves and winds which disturbed your disciples' little boat — 'peace be still'. Amen.

Send us a child

Lord God, you said in days gone by: Go out, increase and multiply — but we can't have a child. Why Lord? We want so much to have a new life to love and cherish. Why Lord? Will you do something about it? We'll go on trying and hoping. Lord do your part.

YOU MUST BE JOKING, LORD

Teach us to be still and attentive

The Psalmist tells us to hold ourselves still before you and wait patiently on you. Lord, teach us how to be still before you when we come to pray. We come so eager to tell you what we'd like you to do and what we'd like, that we are rarely still! We live in a world of constant noise, often imposed on us by others, but frequently through our own choice. We can't relax without the radio! We need to be taught in prayer how to be still with you, and, in life, how to watch attentively so as to discover you in others and in your creation. We need to learn to listen quietly, and patiently, to you in ourselves and in others. Lord, show us how to grow into this attentive, self-forgetting stillness that is part of your peace which is beyond our understanding.

Our prayer group

We have this prayer group, Lord. You know about it, because we get together to be with you, to share, to love each other in you. And it's great. I don't know how to describe what we feel . . . perhaps each of us is different, but we manage to share, to expand to deepen in a way we've never been able to do before. We thank you for this, Lord, and help us to continue growing together, growing in you.

We were happy till they broke in

We were very happy, Lord, till they broke in
and smashed up most of what we had, and beat
us up. Now we can't settle down, we've both
lost our jobs and we're all nervy.
I don't know what we're to do now, Lord.
So I turn to you in complete despair.
I see no way out . . . we're drifting, we're
really lost. Show us the way.

Send us your Spirit of understanding . . .

When we talk together,
we come close together. Then we
get to a point beyond which we don't seem able
to go.
I don't think Lord either of us knows
what goes wrong, what's the barrier.
But we can't go on.
Sometimes, I think we do not know each other enough.
But I think it is a matter of trust.
Sometimes, it seems it is understanding, putting things
    differently
But another time it is just disinterest. It's easier not to
have to bother . . . easier just to be myself.
So what I think we need from you, Lord, is the gift of
your Spirit . . .
of understanding
of love,

of wisdom, of patience, of kindness
. . . send us your Spirit, Lord, send us
your Spirit . . . so that we may really know and love each
other Amen.

The world

I saw a beautiful/horrible TV documentary the other day, Lord. It showed the wonder and grace of your world, growing in a million colours and peopled by birds and fishes, and animals and man. Then it showed the horror — animal preying on animal, fish on fish, bird on bird, man . . . on everything! Is this all necessary? Why, Lord, does it have to be this way, if you are almighty and all-loving?

THEM

We live in a world where it is possible to put a lot of blame on other people or on authority.

'They' are a wonderfully convenient object to abuse, scorn, dislike, irritation and even hate. 'They' are not easy to love.

So, in this section, we try to look at those outside ourselves. We take some of our own feelings as they react to others. We take some of our frustrations and dislikes. But we also take some of our care and concern, the beginnings of our love, and let them grow towards 'Them', so that out of this relationship 'They' may become real.

Quite a lot of our difficulties come from ignorance of each other. We can easily misunderstand; we can be taken up the wrong way; we can take 'an instant dislike' to someone; we can misjudge.

Talking or writing of love, St. Paul says: Love is patient, is kind, never jealous, rude, selfish. Love does not take offence, is not resentful . . . is always ready to excuse, to trust, to hope and to endure whatever comes (I. Cor. 13.).

The demands of Jesus Christ go beyond loving our neighbour . . . Them . . . to loving those who hate us . . . Them.

If these prayers are helpful to you personally, then

they should be accepted as jumping-off places for your own particular need to refer patiently, lovingly, in a caring fashion to each and every person other than yourself.

SHORT PRAYERS

Why do they lie all the time, Lord? I know they are lying, but what am I to do, Lord?

They treat us like pawns, Lord. Teach them we're real!

They keep on making one way streets, but, Lord, I can't keep pace.

They tell me you don't exist. They are more clever than me. But I believe, Lord. Open their eyes. I can't.

Lord, teach me to pray with others as others would pray with me.

Damn! Blast! . . . I just feel this Lord! I know I shouldn't, but THEY get me down, Lord! Do something!

They are full of beauty, full of grace, full of life. Lord, if only we human beings could learn from flowers and animals.

I watched them dancing. They are lovely, Lord. Thank you for the grace of the human body.

They don't understand

I only wanted to go to the disco, Lord. It's perfectly O.K. There's never any trouble. But They say I can't. How stupid they are. Can't parents ever understand, Lord? It seems to me you haven't planned people very well if they make such a mess of their children as I feel Mum and Dad are making of me. All right, Lord, I'll try, but you must try too, or else I'm afraid I won't trust you any more. Sorry, but I mean it, Lord!

'Them' on the motorway

Lord, I try to go slowly and carefully when it's foggy on the motorway, because it's so easy to crash into the car ahead. Please make other people drive considerately too; and help them to understand that this is a form of loving their neighbours as well as looking after themselves!

They hound me

Lord, what can I do when they are hounding me? They scoff and they threaten, and I have no one to turn to. My mother doesn't understand. She thinks I'm imagining things or telling lies so as to get attention. Lord, I'm being hunted and hounded like an animal, and like an animal I'm cowering in fear. I know they're bullies and don't like opposition, so help me to have courage to stand up to them and trust you to defend me as you did when Daniel was hemmed in by the lions in their den. Protect me, save me, Lord!

Parents

Lord, it's impossible to communicate with my Mum and Dad. They don't understand what I'm talking about. They don't see what I do is right for me, in my world. I have to try things out for myself; I can't learn from their experiences, and they don't and won't realise that the world has changed since their youth! I have to learn for myself however scary it may seem to them. Of course it's dangerous, and I may get hurt, and hurt them perhaps, as well as others. I don't want their kind of stuffy security. I want to find out what my life is for, what the world's for. If you exist or whether you're a kind of try-on they've invented to keep us quiet. So if you do exist, help me to live fully and make *them* understand I've got to live and experience things for myself!

City Councillors and politicians

They're no good at all, Lord. They put up the rates, they don't even get the streets swept, the whole town is a mess. Why do we elect them, Lord . . . what is the good of councillors and politicians? I'm fed up with them all. Make them a little more concerned for people and less taken up with their status and committees.

They are trying out pot

Lord give me strength and courage! The gang I go around with are trying out pot and they want me to have a go too. I know it's bad and I know what can happen to kids that get hooked. But, Lord, they say it's fantastic, and I'd just like to know what it feels like! I don't want to be different or miss anything that's going, and, I'm eaten up with curiosity too. Help me not to give in to myself and the others, for the sake of your Son who was tempted to experiment with evil in the desert. Amen.

They say I did it!

Lord, I didn't do it and they say I did. What do I say now? Should I keep saying I didn't do it? They won't believe me. Should I just keep silent like you when you were wrongly accused? It's hard to be silent when you are bursting with the injustice of it! It hurts to be thought guilty when you aren't. Stop me from being bitter and resenting them so much. Help, Lord, help!

Let them be quiet

I just want peace, Lord. That's all I ask. I just want peace. I say to them 'For God's sake, shut up. Be quiet'. I really mean for my sake. So, Lord, for my sake, let them be quiet!

YOU MUST BE JOKING, LORD

They are violent

Lord, I can't understand the violence there is around us today. Innocent people get beaten up in the streets or killed by a bomb in a pub; bodies once full of life are broken and battered. Then I think of your body tortured, mutilated and broken on the cross; it was seemingly useless, but it has given us strength to live more fully and lovingly. Help us, who are your body on earth, to break the power of violence through the strength of the love you give us. Help us to bear the pain and the cost of this loving with courage and joy!

Have they never done wrong?

Lord, it is horrible in this police station and worse visiting a prison . . . all the waiting, the smell, the sense of men and women more as animals. I know he did it, I know he shouldn't have, but he is still a man, Lord . . . he's my man, and father of our children. So why did he have to do it? And now it's done, why do they treat him in this way? Have they never done anything wrong, Lord? Have they not got husbands, wives, children? Why are they so hard? Does all this help him or them to get better? Of course, I don't really know what I would do, but not this, Lord, surely? Anyhow, what I'm asking is that he gets out soon, and that 'they' find a better solution to this problem.

People, people, people.

They say in the North of England:
'Ther's nowt so queer as folk'.
I think they are right, Lord, because
you see I try to be nice to people, and to
understand them. I try to help and
be of service to them. I try to
listen and sympathise . . .
And all I get is a rude word,
a sneer, a demand for more.
You, Lord, talked about ingratitude when
you cured nine lepers and only one said:
Thank you.
Oh, I know this isn't everything, but now I
know how it hurts, how it makes me feel:—
O.K., I'll not try any more to be a neighbour!
But people are your people, so I suppose
in spite of everything,
I'll try to help people,
people, people, Lord . . . your people.

Praying for others

Lord, I don't like praying for others when they really invade my prayer. It's fine having a list and saying their names to you and telling you what you should do for them; then I feel I'm doing something for them. But when their pains and problems really keep interrupting my times of adoration and disturb my sense of my being alone with you and make me realise I'm not in control of the prayer, I don't like it at all!

Lord, is having distractions about people a way of praying for them? Is it your way of showing me how I should give up something so as to share in their distress? Is this how you let me know that you must choose the way I pray and that I must follow your leading? It's very disturbing and uncomfortable. Show me how you want me to pray and teach me to follow your leading and not go on in my own way. Stop me from complaining about the uncomfortableness and untidiness of your way!

Those who care for the disabled

Lord, I want to pray for those who spend their lives looking after the disabled. It is not easy for us to realise how much they have to give up to do this; ambition and high wages have to be put on one side so as to look after people whom many think are useless and shouldn't be kept alive. Lord, help us to understand their devotion and their work. Give them your peace and strength so that they can keep on caring for the disabled lovingly and patiently, and also help them to accept that they will be despised as fools by the go-getters of the world. Teach them to learn from the courage of their patients when they are brave and cheerful, and in turn to be compassionate and understanding when their patients' limbs won't obey their minds even in very small things. Open our eyes to the goodness in others.

For those who attempt suicide

Lord, it is very easy to say of someone who has failed to commit suicide 'they didn't really mean to succeed'. How can we tell? Can we ever start to understand their misery when they discover they are still alive and have to face living all over again. When I'm tired and find life difficult to cope with, I go to bed, and sleep and awake with new energy to start again. This doesn't happen with failed suicides. It's even worse than before, when they come to, because they have to endure the sorrow they've caused to their friends and family. Lord, teach us to be sympathetic with those whose actions we do not understand, and try to appreciate in some way the complete hopelessness that comes with depression. Never let us forget to pray for them.

Children and honesty

Lord, give me wisdom so that I can teach my children about right and wrong, and good and evil, so that when they face the temptations to dishonesty that come even to young school children they will stand firm. It is so easy to lie and cheat at lessons and it can make life easier. Others do it and get away with it and to do things the easy way is such a temptation today. How, Lord, can I show my children that honesty and the hard way with no short cuts, are right, without sounding stuffy and pious? Help me so that I may live in such a way that doing the right thing seems worthwhile.

The homeless

Lord, you had nowhere to lay your head and you said you would judge those who had not fed and clothed you. You meant that if we didn't look after your children, our brothers and sisters, we'd be failing to care for you. Well, Lord, I'm worried about the people today who haven't houses, or have crowded homes where whole families live in one room, or where there is so much noise they can't sleep. What can I do? I can give money to help house people, but how do I encourage others to build houses and to get on with it? How do I stop speculators? The prophets knew all about them and denounced them, but I often wonder if they got anything done about it either! How can I denounce them today in an effective way? Show me, Lord.

Children and loving God

Lord, I want above all to bring up my children to know and love you. It is not easy to explain to them that you love them and care for them, especially when things go wrong and they are hurt physically or wounded mentally. I know I must show my trust in you and go on serenely and lovingly when I too am hurt. Take me over, Lord, completely, rule my life and shine through me with your light so that they may know that you are a living and loving God. Please let me forget myself through loving you, for this is the way that they will grow to see the depth of your love. Help me dear Lord.

Children and evil

Lord, above all I want my children to be honest, and strong to resist evil. Show me how to do this. I know that unless we can trust you and follow your Son, who lived so trustingly and honestly, this is not possible. You alone can teach us the honesty that is so deeply rooted in us that the powers of evil cannot shake it. You alone can give us this foundation. Help me to root and ground my children in you so that by loving you they will not falter in honesty and trust. You only can protect them from evil so give them strength to stand firm, and wrap them about with your love so that they never falter or fail. Help me always to remember to pray for their safe-keeping, O Lord, for you are my strong tower and protection.

The children are bored at church

Lord, I often find church boring. Things are always the same and rarely exciting. Where is your Spirit? How can I expect my children not to be bored too? The words in the services are not always easy to understand, and there is so little movement. They are used to the movement and magic of television, and to music that makes them dance. They have to keep still in church, and the music is so dirge-like and dull that they wouldn't even want to dance. Lord please do something to us so that we can make your worship so joyful that we and our children are caught in the wonder and glory of it, and lifted up by the joy of praising you.

YOU MUST BE JOKING, LORD

When short-tempered with my children

Lord, I've been snapping at the children again because I'm tired and not because they have done anything wrong. I feel so guilty and they look so bewildered when I go for them like this; forgive me, Lord, and help them to forget my bad temper. I feel a failure as a mother and don't know what to do. Please strengthen me and help me to remain patient even when I am exhausted. Teach me how to grow into that deep calm that Jesus had even when he was weary and surrounded by demanding crowds. But now forgive me, and make the children understanding and forgiving too.

Talking to parents

When I was nearly twenty, Lord, I found I could not talk to my mother and father. They wanted to know things and I went all shut up inside. They wanted to find out where I had been, who I was going out with and all the rest. I just couldn't talk to them. And it went on quite some time, with irritation on my side and I think hurt on theirs. But I couldn't open up . . . And now they are both dead, Lord. And I know how much I'd like to have them here to talk to. Let them know this, Lord. And, will you please help all those who are now like I was then . . . help them to talk at home and share with their parents, and help their parents to understand them and not press too hard.

Help others understand me and you

Lord, help others to understand my dark, obscure way of loving you which seems to those who know your Son in a clear way far from right. This wonderful darkness which envelopes me like Moses' cloud is full of you and peace of an elusive kind. It is everything in my life but I can't describe it! describing it can make me doubt; it's a kind of walking on the water, and if I look to see what the water's like I panic and sink. Lord help others to see you reveal yourself in many ways — even in darkness!

Spiders

Heaven knows why you made spiders, Lord. I suppose there is some reason, but I don't see it, because they give me the creeps! Why does anything you made give me the creeps, if you made them and me, and your creation was good? I don't get it, Lord.

Them and their cars

They pour into cities in their cars. They foul up the air and the roads, they use vast quantities of fuel. Why are they so selfish and so stupid, Lord, that they drive into cities in cars?

Visiting them

Lord, why should we waste our Sunday afternoon visiting her parents? It's miserable! We sit around listening to her Dad telling us about the political situation and how much better things were in the old days. I'm not allowed to say a word because my ideas would make him wild! Then when we go home we are both tense because she knows how much I hate going and I can't help showing it. Lord, make me more patient and help me to try to see some good in her father and mother because after all they are your creation, and because I love her. Prevent me from taking my annoyance out on her and making rows about it, and do something to stop us having to go next week.

Race

White man: You'll say I'm a racialist, he said, well so I am, and I think I have a right to be. My Irish forefathers had to sweat their guts out in oppression. There was no Race Relations Act for them. Now any action I take to protect myself and my family is called discrimination. Well, we've fought for what we have got, and I am going to fight not to lose it. I am sure Christ would want me to do that.

Black man: You make my forefather slave; you forbid marriage; you no educate, you say me de scum of de earth, boy, lik me boots, boy, fetch me horse, boy, you

no rights, boy. So I get me a job here, yessir, I get me
house and I have me wife and I fight for me right to be a
man. I a Christian, man. Jesus say all men equal; say do
not oppress poor man, give him food, work, freedom.
So I fight, man, for me family and for me, and I feel de
opposition, de hatred, Lord. And I say 'Lord, set your
people free'.

Everyman: So, Lord, there are these two visions of the
same town, the same street, the same society. And I am
in the middle of it. I want to love you. I want to be
Christian and follow you. But which of these two is
following you, Lord? Or are they both, from different
backgrounds?

Where do I stand, Lord? What do I say, Lord? What
do I do? How can I help to preach what you truly mean
about justice, and brotherly love, about giving and
listening and accepting the cross? Oh dear Lord, help me
because I am battered from every side. All ways I seem
to be wrong. What can I do, what can I say? O, Lord . . .
give me understanding, wisdom, patience, love. Amen.

Institutional churches

Lord, how can you expect me to belong to your
church when I see how often it has persecuted Christians
who were trying to follow Jesus in simple faith? Every
historical series on TV shows Christians of different
kinds being killed by the Church of the time. How can
these persecutors be followers of Jesus? It is impossible to

see that they were showing forth your love to the world.

Lord, it undermines my belief in the institutional churches, yet I love you and want to follow you. I don't know what to do; I can't see how it could be your will that I should belong to an institutional church which has grown from so much hate, fear and blood-shed. Lord, what am I to do and how can I 'show forth' your love in the world? But first take this bitterness and hate of the persecuting church out of my heart, and help me to say 'forgive them for they did not know what they were doing!'

Relating to people like Jesus

Lord, I'd like to be like Jesus who was so fully alive and who related to so many kinds of people and at such depth. He was a noticing person too, seeing things that nobody else paid attention to. He saw the blind beggar at the back of the crowd and little Zachaeus in the branches of the tree and he appreciated their needs. He discovered in a farmer sowing his seed, in a woman looking for a lost coin and in other little things of life, something deep and valuable about God and the world we live in. Help me to grow to have this kind of deep insight into life and people which makes us care for and understand others, and even ourselves, better. Forgive our superficial and unseeing kind of living, for the sake of Jesus who loved and saw deeply into the human heart.

They think marriage stupid

When you talked about marriage and the hardness of it, your disciples, Lord, suggested that if it was to be like that, it would be better not to marry. Today, it seems as though many in the world agree with this, and so they either do not get married, or they come and go with partners, without any idea of saying 'till death do us part'. So, Lord, it is not easy to talk to young people about love which is lasting, about love which will go through hell and come out the other side prepared to go through it again. They think it stupid. If love arrives in hell, that is the time to get out and find another love. But can you teach me, Lord, how I am going to get across to young people, and older ones too, that love has to battle, has to be dreary and dull and sometimes unfeeling, held in place by the will . . . yet eventually coming through into something deeper than before, more real, more beautiful . . . eventually.

Drug-pushers

Lord, I hate drug-pushers! They destroy the kids who fall for their patter. It's terrifying. Sometimes the kids are madly bright and on top of the world, and at others they go limp and pale, and down into the depths. Somehow they become less than human. Why, Lord, have pushers power to destroy and betray others for money? I can't believe that they are human. Perhaps Judas was like that, though I think it was the kingdom, the power and the glory that he was after. Lord, is it bad to get caught by a hate for evil-doers? Perhaps it's my own helplessness that I hate, or the society that won't stop pushers; I don't know. Help me, Lord, to find a way of doing something to stop this awful trade and to prevent children from being taken in by the dangerous attractiveness of drugs!

Motorbikes

God, I love motorbikes. I don't treat them very well. Help me to do better!

The family next door.

We can hear them through the wall . . . they shout and scream at each other. Lord, help them to be a happy family like us.

A wonderful family

I came across a wonderful family, Lord. They did not have very much; a little hovel of a house, a child sick with pneumonia, the husband coughing up his guts, and only bread and marg on the table. But they all had a calm serenity, a love of each other and a great gaiety which infected me. I asked, Lord, why they were so happy. The husband said between coughs: 'The Lord is good:

he does not leave us. We lack many things that others think important. But we have him. Is that not wonderful, a thing of joy'. O Lord, that I had their faith, their hope, their love. Increase my faith!

Sorry for them

Every now and then, a poster or an advert catches my eye. It is not always the same poster, but it is always different from the rest. Most posters say: 'It's the best', 'You must own one', 'Get it today' and so on. This one is often a lined, sad face or a fragile half-naked body, lying emaciated. Generally the picture itself tells all, but on occasions it says underneath 'Feed the hungry' or something like that.

O Lord, it knots my well-filled stomach, it tears at my heart — and yet there is so little I can do against the economy and system of the world in which I live. And worse than that, there is so little I am myself prepared to do, because I like my well-filled stomach and my home; I like T.V. and central-heating and the use of a bus or train or motor car.

So, though a lot of me hates to do this, I'm asking you now Lord, against my better judgment, to waken me and others, and especially our leaders to poverty and famine, to THEIR need, not ours. Teach us the love of Christ, so that we agree to cut back our way of life for them.

Lord, I don't like this prayer, but yet I must pray it against myself for THEM.

YOU MUST BE JOKING, LORD

Worrying about them

I can't help worrying about them, Lord. There they are, my son and my daughter-in-law. So much in love, so young, so inexperienced. I know he means well. He's a good boy. But so young, Lord. He cannot really look after himself. How can he look after her?

Animals

Lord God, Creator, the Bible says you made animals and trees and flowers . . . you saw that what you made was good. Then it says you made man, and what you made was good. So what's happened, Lord? Are you joking? You see, I love animals, and I can't think why human beings are so cruel. Why do we enslave and cage them? How can I learn from you to teach other people to love what you have made . . . nature, all living creatures and mankind?

I saw them smashed on the motorway

Lord, I saw them smashed on the motorway today, father, mother, and three children. Lord, help them all. Stretch out your healing hand . . . and Lord, teach people to drive more carefully. Amen.

Their religion

People are funny, Lord, aren't they? That's the way you made them and, that is what I don't quite understand. If you want them to know you and love you, why make it so hard for them? You see, Lord, anyone with half an eye can understand that football is much more attractive, exciting and important in life than you are ... for millions of people. To go to a mtach is far more moving, far more of an experience than going to church: to sit in front of the TV is enthralling, gripping, real.

But then, Lord, I get more confused, because out of football comes betting, huge hopes built on pools, and growing violence. So what I'm really wondering is whether I'm mad because I cannot understand how it is right for us to be so wrapped up in a game. Or whether they are all sane and sensible, and I'm mad in putting you first?

And then again, I say to myself, can we not do both — have football and God as our religion. O Lord, I wish I knew.

Perhaps you will help by making me understand them and them understand you. I don't know, Lord ... I leave it to you.

YOU—KNOWING YOU IN THE HEART

There comes a time — for some it is 'at once', for some it echoes St. Augustine's 'too late have I loved Thee' — when we realise that our relationship with God does not begin with us.

God is creator — not only of all that is — but also of the knowing-loving relationship between me (man-woman) and Him (God and God-man).

Just as the newborn child is first loved by mother and father, even before the child is conscious of anything except primal instincts of need for food, warmth, comforting . . . so the wonder, as John says, is 'that God has first loved us'.

We grow to realise this.

When we do realise, then our whole attitude is transformed.

No longer do we have to seek anxiously, to sweat at relating to God, at keeping our attention focussed and so on.

Now we begin to know the love of God; the cloud of unknowing things; great shafts of light, gleams of beauty, vistas of wonder strike in upon our consciousness. How, where, why? . . . we do not know.

And yet we do.

Then, in one sense, everything fades or becomes

tasteless except God – You. Heart, mind, body, spirit . . . any and every part is caught up in a loving embrace.

So – if you find this section incoherent – groping – mixing words and wordlessness – singing silently – still – then stay still. Put the book away. Open to the open spaces of God.

You have come alive with His life – there is no need to put anything into words . . . but if there is a word breathed from your depth, this will be the Word, spoken by the Spirit. For you it will be enough to be.

Jesus. Love. God. You. Lord. Father. Almighty. One.

SHORT PRAYERS

The joy of being loved by you, Lord, stills my tongue and loosens my heart for love.

I never really knew what it was to be thankful 'til I felt your forgiveness, Lord. Thank you.

Why is it that when you have broken me, that I can give you to others?

My joy is to know your presence, Jesus. Why do you hide?

I hated you when you let me fall so low. Now I see what you were at, and I marvel at your insight, Lord.

YOU MUST BE JOKING, LORD

You must be joking, Lord

One of your friends, Lord,
has said: that prayer
is the most natural thing
in the world for men and women.
I can't help thinking that's
a joke and if you have really
made us to know and love you
to talk to you and listen —
and you really planned
me to find it natural — then
for me anyhow
you must be joking, Lord.
I kneel down, or sometimes
sit, I begin to think of you, I
use a word or phrase to help me —
next thing I know my mind
is on breakfast, or what
happened yesterday — or how
I can manage to pay those bills.
Then I drag myself back to you
and am restless and bored
till I find again my mind is
on him or her, or home and
work, on the way life treats me
— bother — it seems really very
unnatural for me to pray.
Either I've got it wrong and am
not rightly set — or
you must be joking, Lord

to let a friend of yours
say that.
You must know it's hard and often dull.
You must know my mind
flits about; you must know
everything aches and I shift and
sleep or drift or day-dream
half-the-time.
I don't mind so much – if I
know this is what it is
meant to be, that I have to
work hard, even work hard to
relax –
that I am in your love
and care – so that you are laughing
with me not frowning at me in
my drowsiness.
Reassure me Lord – show me
a glimpse of your laughter and joy.
Then, when I'm stuck, I can say
with truth and new understanding
of the truth,
　　　　You must be joking Lord.

Teach me to pray

I've got this great longing in me. I want to pray, Lord.
Teach me, let me! It just hurts this longing. Lord, I want
to pray!

Lord, this page is my prayer. I sit blankly before you. Fill the blankness of my page or leave it empty, as you will. Amen.

Courage to pray

Lord, give me courage to pray, courage to pray deeply! Let me find the depths that are in me so that I stop living on the surface, and face myself as I am and you as you give yourself to me. Let me understand what dying to self and living to you mean, and give me the courage to die!

Teach me how to be still

Lord, life is hectic! I rush about so much that when I have time to sit down quietly I feel guilty and think that I should be doing something active. Teach me how to be still and silent. Help me to learn to enjoy being with you at peace when I take time off and make me realise that this is more important even than doing things for others. Teach me how to use silence and quietness so as to grow more aware of your constant presence, and not be afraid of meeting myself because you will be there to support and strengthen me. So help me to rest in you and fill me with your deep peace.

O God, O God!

Today, Lord, I wanted to pray. I got myself there. I knelt down. Nothing happened. I sat down. Nothing happened. My head was full of this and that. I did not know what to do, and I found myself saying over and over again: 'God, O God, O God, O God, O God, O God, O God, O God, O God'; so 'O God', this is what I am praying and it does not seem to mean anything . . . and yet it does, because I don't know what you want from me, and I don't know how to give it, and so here I am just being before you Lord, and all I can say is: 'O God, O God, O God'!

Your joy

Lord, help me to remember when things seem hopeless, that you have died and risen, and will triumph through us. I would like to live always with a sense of the joy of the resurrection, but sometimes the pains and sufferings of life seem to over-shadow it. Keep alive a little flame of joy in my heart, and never let the waters of sorrow and pain extinguish it. Forgive me if I waver a little; it's only temporary, for I know that no sorrow, danger or pain can take this inner joy and elation from me, because you, my redeemer live and I live with you!

The sun is shining

The sun is shining . . . thank you Lord.
I mean it is shining: the sky and everything is
warm and smiling.
But it is not only that . . . my heart is smiling.
I know that I am loved . . . and that I love too.
Thank you, Lord, the sun is shining.

It's raining

It's raining; it's cold; I feel very lonely ... but I love you, Lord.

Make me a channel of your peace

Lord, I want to be a channel of your peace and bring your love to those who hate, as St. Francis' prayer suggests but I don't know how to start!

Help me, Lord, to give myself to you in trust for I feel if I can let go of myself, you will be better able to use me. The trouble is, Lord, that I like being in control and doing things my way, but now I'm saying 'take me and use me as you want'. Give me grace and strength not to go back on my word, because I'll be tempted to! Amen.

Thank you

As I saw the sun set across the beauty of the sky, I looked down to the earth ... chimneys, gasworks, railway lines, slum dwellings, people in the rain. And I wondered which was more beautiful for you? In some funny way, I can see that people in the rain and gasworks and the things you have allowed mankind to make are perhaps even more beautiful to you than the things you made directly. You love these things because they come from the creativity of man, which 'extends' your creativity.

You love man in the rain, because your son was a man in the rain. And before that you had made man to your image and likeness, including a bit of your creativity. Thank you, Lord.

Holy Spirit, help me to decide

Holy Spirit help and guide me. I don't know which choice to make; both are possible and both are good. I want to know which is God's will. Help me to clear my mind so that I will see without prejudice; increase my love so that my choice will be guided by love of you. I am confused and need guidance. When, with your aid, I have chosen, stop me from looking back with regret and give me courage to go on fearlessly, trusting that I have done what is right and what is your will. Amen.

It's great

I could jump and laugh and cry and shout all at once, Lord. It's great, wonderful, marvellous. O thank you and thank you and thank you.

Before you

Here I am before you, take me. If I am distracted, at least take the time I offer!

Your Spirit blows!

The wind's blowing, it's a gale though they call it a breeze here! Yesterday everything was still. Your mysterious Spirit is like that too. Sometimes it is a still, small voice peacefully stirring my inmost heart, and then it is harsh, persistent, battering at me, not letting me rest, driving me on when I'd like to be still. I thank you for your gale, your Spirit, though it is most disrupting!

Your love

Lord, I don't know how to tell people about you and your love. I love you, but I don't understand how it happened! Sometimes, even now, in my mind, I wonder if you exist, and when people pull the gospels to bits, I wonder if Jesus is your son. What did he preach? He said 'follow me' and 'I am the way', but I can't explain how and why he is the way! But then I can't explain how and why I love people or how I know they love me. Lord, you are my life . . . help me to explain how and why, because this knowledge is so wonderful that I want to share it.

Your Spirit

Lord, help me to believe that your Spirit is in my heart; that when I pray your Spirit will help me; that he will show me what to do and what to say in difficult situations; that he will lead me to show forth your glory to the world and to preach the good news of Jesus. O Holy Spirit, teach me to follow you wherever you lead, however rough the path may be, for since you go to and fro' like the wind, your way will be unpredictable and not easy for me, for I love security so much!

Praying in the bath

There is no time for being relaxed, as far as I am concerned, like the time when I am lying in the bath. Some people whistle and sing; some people read, some are just quick in and out. Well, Lord, I find this is a time of peace when I can as it were soften up, let go the tensions, and so let my mind and spirit rise up to you with the steam from the water. I suppose I'm funny praying like this, Lord, but it is a time when I really can thank you for so much, feel lightened and be responsive to you. Thank you Lord, for hot water, peace and prayer.

Lord I am empty

Lord, I am empty. I thought I loved you and that I was growing more like you. Now I find I have nothing only emptiness, and you seem nowhere near me. I realise more than ever before that I am nothing without you. Flow into my emptiness and fill me with your fullness, dear Lord.

You listen

I am glad that I have you to talk to Lord, because you listen and don't tell me to be quiet because you're busy the way Mum does. It's really dreadful to have no one to listen when I have so many interesting things to tell and to say. You are a great help Lord, and Gran is too, as she has time to listen. But then she isn't around very often but you are always with me. I do thank you for being about, but wish you could make Mum less busy so that she could be quiet and interested when I want to talk to her.

Thank you for stilling my prayer

Lord, when I come to pray I know that you are with me and that I should leave the praying to you and be still, but there are so many things to be prayed for that I can't keep quiet! Then suddenly there is a hush, and I know you are praying in me, almost despite me, and it is quite wonderful! Thank you for letting me know this and for experiencing the joy of forgetting myself, and for being taken over by you even for this short moment.

Trusting you

Lord, I know that Daniel wasn't hurt by the lions when he was shut in with them because he trusted you. I wish I had his trust! The world is in chaos, and my life is

147

upset too, and I am afraid for the world and for myself.

In my utter helplessness I turn to you because there is no one else to go to! Christ alone can help us now. Strengthen my weak faith and give me courage and hope, for surely my lions are not as fierce as Daniel's? If the world, and I, have your support, and are in your caring hands, what harm can come to us for you have overcome death and hell, and every other sort of fear?

After prayer

Lord, the fullness of the prayer you gave me makes me long to live with you like this always — you are the thing I long for beyond all others. Let me not lose this sense of you as I now plunge into my daily life!

Let me see you!

Lord, it is difficult to relate to you because I can't see you or touch you. It isn't easy to know that you are here; yet sometimes you seem very close, and like your disciples, my heart burns within me though I'm not sure why! Moses saw you in some strange ways; in a cloud and you spoke to him from a bush! He couldn't touch the cloud, hold it in his hands and look at it; and the bush was burning but not burnt away, frightening and holy.

I'm not sure what all this means to me except you can

reveal yourself in some strange ways, in nature and in life, and that we can't hold on to you or possess you.

Keep me open to your comings; show me how to prepare a way for you in my life, and teach me to rejoice in the mystery and wonder of your ways.

Your silence

Fill the bottomless pit of my emptiness, Lord, from the pools of your silence.

Your peace

Lord, it is good just to be with you in stillness. Your peace soaks into me and all the troubles of life get transformed most wonderfully. Why are all my times with you not like this? I do not forget the troubles of the world and of my friends, but they too are caught in the warmth of your peace, and surely like me, they must be changed by the beauty of it.

You hang there triumphant

Lord, looking at the cross today, I don't see its revoltingness, but only your heroic courage. This transforms the horror of the cross, the beastliness and the agony of it into something that is dignified and royal. Your persistent love and your forgiveness turns this ghastly instrument of torture and death into a symbol of hope. The pain does not let go, nor does our pain leave us, but your courage changes it and makes it bearable because of your heroic love. I see now, Lord, why they say you reign from the cross, and that in this we triumph! Amen.

You are beyond imagination

Lord, sometimes when I pray, I wonder whether I should be finding words and images, then it comes to me that though my way is beyond images, it is not beyond love. Perhaps it's an odd kind of love, but it is a tenacious kind of cleaving to you, which somehow melts me and takes me beyond myself. You sometimes seem to fill it with wonder, joy and peace, and at others you fill it with emptiness and sorrow for my sin. Lord, never let me doubt that it is prayer, for it is what you give me.

You are wonderful

Lord, you are wonderful beyond all words, all thoughts, all emotions, all imaginings!

You are more wonderful than anything that I have ever known. You are stillness, you are wayless, you are light, you are joy, you are the fullness of all things — yet you are more wonderful than all these! If only there were words to express what you are, if there were images to

describe you or music to suggest the magic of your being!
All descriptions are only smudged shadows of your
reality.

You are wonderful beyond all things and yet you have
touched me with yourself so that I have glimpsed the
wonder, the greatness, the mysteriousness of you which
are beyond description!

You pray in me

Some time ago I began to try to pray to you, Lord.
I didn't really know how, so I just began by asking
for things I thought I wanted.
But afterwards, something began to happen. It
wasn't that you gave me what I asked, but somehow
that seemed unimportant. It was
as though I suddenly understood – something.
I was walking along, not thinking and
suddenly everything was golden and at peace.
For the first time I heard a bird singing,
while the sun reflected off the factory chimney
with the effect of bricks ablaze.
I stood, and there was stillness . . . it wasn't
that the city noise had stopped, but
there was a stillness in the midst,
as it were, the eye of the storm, serene
though all around there was a buffeting of sound,
of movement and of competition.
But I was still too – still in the
depth of me – alone,

and yet committed to the noisy world around —
dwelling among men — in the midst — with —
Perhaps, Lord, at this point I knew,
for the first time,
that it was not I who pray,
but your Spirit who prays in me saying —
Father,
and in that word, stilling the noisy world to
peace,
as a child is stilled by daddy, in his arms, secure,
loving and being loved — knowing love — enfolded.
So now I know, in a small way, that even I can pray.
because I am a man, and so you pray in me.
I used to think that this was only for the great,
for monks and nuns and saints, but now I know,
you take in every man and woman, you enfold every child
in your love, so each of us
can pray,
if only we let you pray in us.
And so I thank you, Lord, which is better than just
     asking,
and I almost burst with the incredible fact —
You love me, you care for me, and I love you, a little
     now,
and later perhaps a little more, until . . .
well, Lord, I haven't got there yet, but thank you, Lord,
that such as me can pray, because you pray in me.
Thank you. Amen.

Unutterable love

There is a time when everything stops –
suspended.
It could be called being 'in the Lord',
couldn't it, Lord?
Caught, held, loved – what word can I use?
This, Lord, is a sense under every other sense,
a realisation above all other realisations . . .
But what can human word mean in explanation?
You spoke your Word, Lord, and a man called Paul
tried to express the inexpressible you –
'O the depths of the riches and wisdom and knowledge
of God! How unsearchable are his judgments and
how inscrutable are his ways!'
A man called Thomas Aquinas wrote many volumes
about you . . . and then said it was so much dust
compared with the 'experience of you'.
Lord, I know that experience, and I want to voice it,
shout it . . .
but no word comes,
because the wonder is utterly inexpressible –
so inexpressible I ache with it, long with it,
a woman called Teresa of Avila swooned with it . . .
Love of my life, Life of my love, Lord – Almighty –
Wonder – awe – LOVE – You . . .
Thank you! Amen.

INDEX

Adopted, 41
Alone, 52
Anger, 49, 70
Animals, 67, 92, 134
Attentive, make us, 112
Attractive, I'd like to be, 62

Baby, my, 83, 94
Bad thoughts, 49
Baptism, 100
Bath, praying in the, 146
Belief, 17
Bitchy, 63
Black and white love, 108

Cat, my, 92
Careers, 44
Children, ours, 123-126
Church, 95, 97, 129
Councillors, 118
Country, visiting the, 63
Crisis, 78
Cross, understanding the, 18, 149

Dead person, seeing a, 67
Depressed, 71

Dog, fear of,   67
      run over,   92
Driving test,   91
Drugs,   119, 131
Drunk,   73

Elections,   77
Empty, I'm   66, 146
Evil, fear of,   69, 125
Exams,   50, 51
Excuses,   74

Families,   132
Father,   18, 58, 89
Fear,   52, 62, 66
Fire,   67
Forgetting,   75
Forgiving,   87, 111

Grandmother,   95
Growing up,   47
God, throughout the book

Hate,   51, 94
Holy Spirit,   144, 145
Homeless, the,   124
Hounded,   117
Housekeeping accounts,   92
Humour,   110
Husband,   89, 90, 99

Identity, my, 39, 40
Instant Christians, 107

Jealous, 84
Jesus, 28, 29 and throughout the book
Job, that I want 78
Joy, 142

Loneliness, 62
Lord's Prayer, 107
Love, 20, 24, 53, 55, 86, 88, 108, 145, 153
Lovable, 73, 98

Marriage, 56, 103, 131
Mother, 83, 96, 97, 98, 102
Mother-in-law, 105
Motorway, 76, 117, 134

Parents, 117, 118, 126, 128
Patience, 74, 95
Peace, 29, 111, 119, 143, 149
People, 52, 121
Pill, the, 54
Place to pray, 20
Prayer, 21, 31, 109, 139, 140, 141, 147, 148, 150, 151
    no answer to, 25
    prayer group, 112
Praying for others, 121, 122, 123
Policeman's prayer, 27, 64
Pop-star, 87
Problem of being me, 36

Purpose in life, 36

Quarrel, 85, 105, 106
Questioning God, 34 and in many other places

Race relations, 108, 128, 129
Rain, 86, 143
Relating, 70, 112, 130

Scared, 52, 66, 67, 69, 96
School, 44, 45, 46
Science fiction, 23
Self-centred, 108
Sex, problems, 55, 56, 57
Silence, God's, 149
Sleep, 66
Soldier's prayer, 60
Spiders, 127
Spot, a, 54
Stealing, 74, 76
Still, teach me to be, 141
Sunshine, 142
Superficial living, 104

Teenager, no longer, 59
Telly, quarrelling about, 105
Thanksgiving, 21, 22, 23, 63, 143, 144
Theft, 113
Tomorrow, 68
Trusting God, 19, 147

Unbelief, 17
Understanding God, 127
Unmarried, 77
Untidy, 54

Values, 104
Violence, 75, 120

Waiting, 51
Weary, 71
Wife, 93
Wonder of God, 150
World, God's, 111, 114
Work, 51
Worrying, 133, 134